BOOK OF

CHRISTIAN ESCHATOLOGY

— STUDY OF THE END TIMES —

• STUDY 2 •

PRAYER M. MADUEKE

PRAYER
PUBLICATIONS
UNITED STATES

ISBN: 979-8691155697

Published by **Prayer Publications**

259 Wainwright Street, Newark,

New Jersey 07112 United States.

From the Author

Prayer M. Madueke

CHRISTIAN AUTHOR

My name is Prayer Madueke. I'm a spiritual warrior in the lord's vineyard. An accomplished author, speaker and expert on spiritual warfare and deliverance. I've published well over 100 books on every area of successful Christian living. I'm an acclaimed family and relationship counselor with several of titles dealing with those critical areas in the lives of the children of God. I travel to several countries each year speaking and conducting deliverance, breaking the yokes of demonic oppression and setting captives free.

I will be delighted to partner with you also in organized crusades, ceremonies, marriages and marriage seminars, special events, church ministration and fellowship for the advancement of God's kingdom here on earth.

All my books can be found <u>Amazon.com</u>. Visit my website <u>www.madueke.com</u> for powerful devotionals and materials.

Free Book Gift

Just to say Thank You for getting my book: Christian Eschatology –

Study 2, I'll like to give you these books for free:

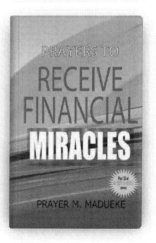

The link to download them are at the end of this book.

Your testimonies will abound. <u>Click here</u> to see my other books. They have produced many testimonies and I want your testimony to be one too.

Prayer Requests or Counselling

Send me an email on <u>prayermadu@yahoo.com</u> if you need prayers or counsel or you have questions. Better still if you want to be friends with me.

Table of Contents

CHAPTER ONE

SIXTH LETTER

DELIVERANCE FROM CORRUPTION

Revelation 3:7-13

Philadelphia church is the only church among the seven churches in Asia that received one of the seven letters written by Christ who was praised by Christ. Christ blessed them for being loyal and faithful. In Christ's letter, He introduced Himself as one that is holy, true and He that has the key of David.

'And to the angel of the church in Philadelphia write; These things saith he that is holy, he that is true, he that hath the key of David, he that openeth, and no man shutteth; and shutteth, and no man openeth; I know thy works: behold, I have set before thee an open door, and no man can shut it: for thou hast a little strength, and hast *kept my word, and hast not denied my name' (Revelation 3:7-8).*

Philadelphia, the city of brotherly love was founded by the king of Pergamos by 140 BC and named after the king. It was situated about 28 miles southeast of Sardis. It was rich in agriculture, though beset by constant earthquakes. The city still exists today under a different name that means city of God. This city of Asia Minor had a faithful, true church that followed Jesus Christ whole-heartedly. There was no corruption in their doctrine, worship or practice. Consequently, Christ had no correction or condemnation for them. This church was unique and different from all others in Asia Minor. It was a Christ-honoring church.

'For he hath made him to be sin for us, who knew no sin; that we might be made the righteousness of God in him' (2 Corinthians 5:21).

'For we have not an high priest which cannot be touched with the feeling of our infirmities; but was in all points tempted like as we are, yet without sin' (Hebrews 4:15).

When Christ introduced Himself to them, He presented His righteous nature, the truth, the one that has the final authority, He that opens and no man shuts and shuts, no man opens. Christ has sovereign and ultimate power, He is true and faithful which the key symbolizes. He has all authority to rule, reign do and undo at will.

'And to the angel of the church in Philadelphia write; These things saith he that is holy, he that is true, he that hath the key of David, he that openeth, and no man shutteth; and shutteth, and no man openeth' (Revelation 3:7).

He is the righteousness of God and the detail of divine purity. He humbled Himself, born in the flesh, experienced human weakness and all infirmities and become our High Priest. He faced every trial, tests and human limitation for our sake and in all point passed through whatever anyone had passed through, is passing through and will ever pass through. He knows what you are going through and is ready to help you come out of it victorious. No one has any excuse left for him to sin and deny faith because Christ is ready to deliver us. In His introduction to the holy and true church in

Philadelphia, He manifested as the Holy, True and Authoritative one, the source of their strength, holiness and faithfulness. He has the key of every good thing, key to salvation, truth, holiness, deliverance, power to serve Him and the key to opportunities. No believer can do without Him and all unbelievers are counted as failure because any success without Christ is useless and as good as nothing.

'Jesus saith unto him, I am the way, the truth, and the life: no man cometh unto the Father, but by me' (John 14:6).

'I am the vine, ye are the branches: He that abideth in me, and I in him, the same bringeth forth much fruit: for without me ye can do nothing' (John 15:5).

'I am the door: by me if any man enter in, he shall be saved, and shall go in and out, and find pasture' (John 10:9).

His introduction is pointing to His direction as overall and the best of the bests. To ignore Him is to reject life and accept death. If you leave Christ, you will miss your way in life and your end will be disastrous. To claim to be righteous, prove to be holy without relationship with Christ is a deceit. Every holiness, righteous living and purity is from Christ. If you want to do anything right, get anything right, you must have relationship with Christ.

There are believers, ministers and people who are so inpatient in life, so they go ahead of Christ to get good things and come back to serve Christ without true repentance and restitution. That is a deceit because, no matter how much you serve Him with those good things, they are not accepted. Many ministers ran faster than Christ and pursued power for service. They despised the laid down rules for true power for service. They break God's laws, move ahead of time set for them for power and receive fake power from evil authority.

They have zeal to work for God, help the needy, the poor, prophesy, cast out devil and do many wonderful things for Christ in their heart, they are sincere to serve God but they went ahead of their time for service and empowerment. Their ways are perverse, defiled and filled with demons. They got what they wanted from the wrong side. They came back, start ministry, prophesy in the name of Christ, preach in the name of Christ and everything they do, they do in the name of Christ.

In their mind, they believe that they are working for God, they think they are pleasing God. But the truth is that, they are deceived and they operate under the influence of demons. They believe that they are casting out demons. The truth is that such people are not casting out demons. They are in covenant with evil spirit to transfer demons, postpone satanic activities and suspend demonic actions for a while.

'Not everyone that saith unto me, Lord, Lord, shall enter into the kingdom of heaven; but he that doeth the will of my Father which is in heaven. Many will say to me in that day, Lord, Lord, have we not prophesied in thy name? And in thy name have cast out devils? And in thy name done many wonderful works? And then will I profess unto them, I never knew you: depart from me, ye that work iniquity' (Matthew 7:21-23).

There are small boys and girls, very young in ministry, without any guiding spiritual father or training filled everywhere with cloud following them. They are under the yoke of the devil; they are deceived to deceive others. They have no training, no guide and no character or respect, yet they rushed into ministry. It is very dangerous and destructive to rush into ministry without character, the fruit of the Spirit.

'Envyings, murders, drunkenness, revellings, and such like: of the which I tell you before, as I have also told you in time past, that they which do such things shall not inherit the kingdom of God. But the fruit of the Spirit is love, joy, peace, longsuffering, gentleness, goodness, faith' (<u>Galatians 5:21-22</u>).

When I look into many young ministers' ministries, I pity the multitudes following them, why? They are in business with the devil to deceive their followers, merchandise them and make them enemies of Christ. They are filled with the spirit of subtlety, mischief and perversion. They are enemies of righteous living, children of the devil without the fruits of the Spirit. They are empowered by the devil to transfer problems from head to leg, liver to kidney, brain to intestine, etc. If you sow more seed, pay them more tithes direct for personal use, they can transfer your problems to your wife, husband, children, other places or business.

To the devil and his ministers, you must never be free. By the time they finish with you and you do not have anything to give, you will be abandoned to die. Most people like that get offended at God, blame God, find fault and die in their sins to spend eternity in hell fire. That is why you pray many prayers, go for many deliverance but will never be delivered. Other deceived ministers can postpone your problem or suspend them. They are in covenant with the devil and they are empowered to do so. They can never cast out demons because demons cannot cast out demons.

Every program they organize is to make more money, deceive people and increase demonic activities. It is very difficult to discover some of them because they practice fake holiness and try to do good, help widows to deceive many. If you come too close to them and discover their secret, you become an object of their attacks.

Some of them can pray very well, fast and preach soundly but everything they do is defiled. They try to imitate every good thing that Christ do but looking very close, they are counterfeit of Satan. They have confused the mind of many who desire to serve God. They are false apostles, deceitful workers transforming themselves into the apostles of Christ.

'For such are false apostles, deceitful workers, transforming themselves into the apostles of Christ. And no marvel; for Satan himself is transformed into an angel

of light. Therefore, it is no great thing if his ministers also be transformed as the ministers of righteousness; whose end shall be according to their works' (2 Corinthians 11:13-15).

Our generation is witnessing unprecedented explosion of false ministers in cults. The two problems they have created now are: 1. Some people are already deceived to believe that every supernatural thing is from God and such can easily be deceived by this cult ministers. 2. Others who have been deceived by so-called miracle workers are already so disappointed that right now, they group everything supernatural as counterfeit. They think, believe and teach that real miracles cannot happen anymore in answer to prayer and deliverance programs. They two are deceived. I want to assure you that there are genuine, life-saving, pure miracles from God through the operation of the gifts of the Holy Ghost. You must be careful and prayerful to distinguish and identify the lying wonders of Satan, which he performs through his messengers to deceive the hearts of men and women.

'And he doeth great wonders, so that he maketh fire come down from heaven on the earth in the sight of men, And deceiveth them that dwell on the earth by the means of those miracles which he had power to do in the sight of the beast; saying to them that dwell on the earth, that they should make an image to the beast, which had the wound by a sword, and did live. And he had power to give life unto the image of the beast, that the image of the beast should both speak, and cause that as many as would not worship the image of the beast should be killed' (<u>Revelation 13:13-15</u>).

If you want to know the truth, fake ministers, you must be born again and bear the fruits of the Spirit. Any demonstration of power, show of anointing and prosperity without the grace to live holy is fake. If you have power without purity, discernment, faith, healing anointing and prophetic voice without discipline, holiness and control over your tongue, you are far from God. Many ministers have great gifts and talents that men revere, yet those ministers are under the condemnation of God.

When Christ sent the letter to Philadelphia, He introduced Himself as He that is holy, true with final say. The best thing that will happen to anyone on earth is to identify with Christ. If you do that now, today, He will empower you with the Spirit of holiness, truth and give you access to other things. You cannot ignore Christ, leave Him behind, ignore His righteousness and truth, pursue power, come back, and say you are serving Him.

You may be in a hurry to open ministry, seek and get power by all means but you cannot force Christ to approve your ministry. There are ministers who only know parts of the scriptures that favor their part of ministry and ignore others. Others know the scripture very well but they are faulty in explaining them. Others, because of their intellectual attainment, the conscious of their social class in the society, their wealth often restrain them from knowing the truth. The truth is that no man's wealth, education or position in life is complete if he does not know the scriptures.

Those who fight God's word, misuse God's word, misinterpret God's word, and do evil at the peril of their own soul. In all service, you render to God, preaching and teaching of God's word, the practical aspect, obeying His words is the climax. If you want anything good that will last to eternity and give you everlasting joy, peace and happiness, Christ is the key. His message to the church in Philadelphia is, I am the truth, the way to true power and authority over demons.

His holiness makes you holy, keeps you holy, and leads you to the truth and gives you key into every good thing. If you ignore His words, righteous living and pursue power, deliverance or any other thing, you cannot come back to get His holiness or work in truth unless you abandon the latter. He is a jealous God and cannot accept second-class position. What Christ is demanding from many deceived ministers, believers is to drop whatever they got wrongly.

Drop your position, your power, remove every evil relationship, break evil covenant and seek for real power. He has the key to every good thing but you have to drop everything you got in wrong ways and enter into his way, truth and life. Some ministers need to close up their ministry, become an ordinary member somewhere else before their deliverance will start. Others need to allow the devil to take away their wealth, position for their deliverance to come.

The truth is that many born again are not born again, many salvations are not sanctified, and their Holy Ghost baptisms are not baptized. Jesus wrote to Philadelphia church and told them not to mind or jealous what they see and hear in other churches. He wrote to them and declares Himself as the source of holiness, the true truth that is with the real key of greatness.

The real key to true power, prosperity and access to every need of man in earth and in heaven is with Him. He told them that He has the sovereignty and ultimate power to all powers and authority. He told them, I am the source of strength, holiness and faithfulness. He is the door and by Him, you can enter into salvation, true salvation, and everlasting salvation and can find anything you need in Him.

He told them to remain in faith, to depend on the vine, abide in Him, so that they can bear fruit that will last. He told them not to worry, border, envy or go after ministers who are on the other side. The branch of Christ, His followers cannot make it without remaining in Him. He told them to fight on, keep living right, and wait until they are empowered by Him, before they start. He encouraged them not to go, run or out run Him.

He told them in the letter that He is the access door to greatness for those who will remain faithful to the end. At that time of the letter, many on Philadelphia were righteous but He told them to keep it up. Hold fast what they have, depend on His grace, stand and rejoice in the hope of the coming of the glory of God. While others are rejoicing in their ill-gotten wealth, ministry, fake power, abundance in everything, Christ told the contending believers, that theirs are on the way.

They should not get weak in faith but that they should take their stand to the end. Some of them were in need, but they must not allow those needs to take them away from the grace. They must keep standing, praying, believing God for their deliverance. They must rejoice in hope of their coming testimony, provision, healing, empowerment and the glory of God in their lives. They must never think of going back or looking back.

'By whom also we have access by faith into this grace wherein we stand, and rejoice in hope of the glory of God' (Romans 5:2).

'For through him we both have access by one Spirit unto the Father' (Ephesians 2:18).

'In whom we have boldness and access with confidence by the faith of him' (Ephesians 3:12).

They must wait because very soon their case file with God the father will soon receive approval and release to every of their request for deliverance, anointing and prosperity is about to come from God the father. If you ever get anointing, empowerment, healing and deliverance from God, you will never be intimidated again. You will be bold because your access to re-empowerment and increase will be everlasting. Your boldness and confidence in God will never again be questioned or disengaged. You will be permanently with God's power and anointing for victory in every contest as long as you abide in Christ.

Your power, boldness before the devil and every problem will be permanently permanent. The knowledge that God is with you gives boldness and keeps you fearless before any problem. To be informed that the one that is holy without any defilement is your God is enough to keep you in boldness before any Goliath. To know and be assured by Christ's letter that the one that will lead to the truth, the source of every truth without lies is your Savior is enough to keep you bold before any present problem. To read this letter from Christ assuring you that He who has the key of David, He that opens and no man shuts, and shuts and no man opens is the one standing by you with a letter is enough to give you hope. You will not die in this your problem if you are with such a person, Christ.

Someone who will not hide the truth, which will set you free, should be trusted. Someone who will tell you the truth that no doctor is aware of should be trusted. The one with the truth that will cause your pains to stop, end your hardship and deliver you from destruction should be believed in. Christ has the power, every authority to promote you, bless you and empower you for service. The brethren in Philadelphia were determined to wait for Him, pray until their deliverance comes from Him. They were deadly committed to live holy, remain loyal and faithful to the end. What is your decision for Christ?

CHAPTER TWO

REASONS FOR PRAISE

Revelation 3:10

The believers in Philadelphia were commended for using their little strength to serve God, keep God's Word and honor the name of Christ.

'Unto me, who am less than the least of all saints, is this grace given, that I should preach among the Gentiles the unsearchable riches of Christ' (Ephesians 3:8).

'To the intent that now unto the principalities and powers in heavenly places might be known by the church the manifold wisdom of God' (Ephesians 3:10).

When they got born-again, they received little measure of Christ's strength and they used it for Christ without diverting it. They lived their lives for Christ, pleasing Him with their little strength at every giving opportunity. They were crucified for Christ, dead for Christ and everything in it. They considered that without Christ's sacrifice on the cross, they would have died or be dead in sin. With this in their minds, they decided that the rest of their life on earth must be to please Christ and not self or others. By the time they received Christ's letter, they were living for Christ and Christ praised them for that.

'I am crucified with Christ: nevertheless I live; yet not I, but Christ liveth in me: and the life which I now live in the flesh I live by the faith of the Son of God, who loved me, and gave himself for me' (Galatians 2:20).

'Finally, my brethren, be strong in the Lord, and in the power of his might' (Ephesians 6:10).

With their little strength, they were able to serve God without corruption. With their little strength, they were able to remain holy, faithful and loyal to Christ. With their little amount of money, they used it to serve God and managed to maintain faith. With little offering money, tithes and seed of faith, they remained calm to serve Christ with their little resources. They managed to serve God with little strength in their health; they never looked for healing from the devil.

With their little power, their ministers never went to the devil to look for power. They waited until the day Christ wrote to them. With their tribe's men and women among them, they avoided tribalism, selective judgment or racism. With their little strength, they love God, loved each other, prayed together and trusted God. With their little power, they ignored the false prophets, the prophetess and rejected their prophecies. With their little resources, they met the needs of their members.

With their little resources, they depended upon God, prayed for provision and trusted God to the end. With their little strength, they overcame every enemy; persecutors, lived above division, tribal difference and maintained peace. With their little strength, they overcame their differences, loved each other, pray for the weak and cared for the fatherless. With their little strength, they were bold; they faced every problem together and overcame them. With their little strength, they faced and conquered big troubles, storms of life and afflictions.

With their little strength, they faced every opposition, temptations, Jezebels and kept God's standard. With their little strength, they preached sound gospel, stood against false teachings, doctrines and immorality. With their little strength, they rejected evil relationship, said no to evil associations and unequally yokes. With their little strength, they refused to be corrupted, defiled or sacrifice to idols. With their little strength, they rejected heresies, sexual sins and problems associated with wrong marriages.

With their little strength, they refused to permit wicked relatives to defile holy altars, lead others or control God's finances. With their little power, small strength, they refused to be seduced by immoral women, evil men and deceivers. With their little strength, they overcame evil influence, immoral lifestyles and misleading agents of the devil. With their little strength, they refused to faint under the pressures of sin. With their little strength, they maintained relationship with one another, with Christ and practiced self-denial. With their little strength, they refused to convert the church to social club, entertainment arena and evil competition for display of wealth. Most of them were not educated, rich, greatly anointed but whatever they had was dedicated to God without a minus.

'And he must needs go through Samaria' (John 4:4).

They were strong in the Lord with their little strength, not in witchcraft, false prophesy or fighting one another. Not in waste, stealing God's money or building personal kingdom. Their strength was small, very little, but they managed it and used it to serve God, used what they had to please only God. Their strengths, promotions, wealth's, transfers did not come from charms, witch doctors, occult group or from demon possessed godfathers.

With little strength, they were strong in the Lord and in the power of His might. They never despised that little strength because they knew it came from God. That little strength was small but it is greater than the power in the whole world put together. Any gift you receive from God is greater in quality and quantity than every other thing in this world. If you receive a little power from God, it is greater, bigger and better than every other power on earth. You can overcome the devil, his agents and all the problems of this world with any little power from God.

You can overcome any problem, any mountain, and every opposition with a little power from God. You are richer, better, greater than the whole world with a little measure of God's strength.

'Because the foolishness of God is wiser than men; and the weakness of God is stronger than men' (1Corinthians 1:25).

It is an insult to God to say or believe that anything from Him is small or too little to bring your deliverance. God's foolishness without His wisdom at all, is better than the best wisdom on earth. Any wisdom that the devil can offer you is more foolish than a little foolishness from God. God's worst is far better than the wisdom of the devil put together.

A believer that chose to operate on earth with the smallest foolishness of God is better than all the wisdom of devil on earth put together. The men or women of wisdom you seek for their help in watch doctor's altars, occult altars and all dark kingdom are agents of the devil. Whatever they can give you is lighter than nothing to compare with the foolishness you can receive from God. If you chose to operate only on God's foolishness in this earth, you are far better than any man or woman serving the devil.

Devil's wisdom gathered, heaped upon one single occult group is far less when compared to God's smallest foolishness. No wonder, God said, my people perish for lack of knowledge. If you are looking for power to make wealth, become rich, perform miracles, heal the sick and solve every problem on earth, they are with God. Supposing you fail to get God's power, you can get His weakness.

God's weakness is stronger than the strongest of men that serve the devil. Pastors, minister who go to satanic agents, occult group, and witchcraft groups are the most foolish creature on earth. It is better to look for God's weakness or foolishness than to look for the whole power of the devil. If such pastors, ministers or believers ever were born again, they are under deceit. This is because little strength Christ talked about is the power of salvation.

> *'I know thy works: behold, I have set before thee an open door, and no man can shut it: for thou hast a little strength, and hast kept my word, and hast not denied my name... Because thou hast kept the word of my patience, I also will keep thee from the hour of temptation, which shall come upon all the world, to try them that dwell upon the earth' (Revelation 3:8, 10).*

The little strength in this passage is the initial power a sinner receives in the day he repents. It is called the power of salvation. This power cuts a sinner from sin and from the world at salvation. This was the only power the believers in Philadelphia used to overcome every problem. Their ministers exposed them to the fruits of the Spirit and how to become ambassadors of Christ on earth. They were taught on how to be servants to each other, servant to God, a builder of God's kingdom, a chosen vessel, a steward and ministers.

They were taught on how to forsake sin, Satan and self to follow the Savior. They were led to turn away from darkness to walk in the light. They were taught about the narrow gate, encouraged to enter narrow gate, how to walk in the narrow way. To walk worthy of the vocation where with they were called, they chose to follow the narrow way. They were taught on how to walk in good relationship with one another in their church, at home in the society.

In Philadelphia, the ministers, leaders, bishops taught them about lowliness, meekness, longsuffering, forbearance, love, unity with the church, one another, peace among themselves. They were taught to examine themselves at all times, daily, with their wives, husbands, fellow believers, parents, children, neighbors, co-workers and others in the light of the scriptures. They were taught step by step, without a rush and were given the opportunity to put them in practice. They know these things before going into the school of prayer, ministry, and deliverance.

The ministers in Philadelphia church ministered deliverance on them, proved them as saved, sanctified, holy with the little strength they have before giving them positions in the church. Other ministers ignored the teachings on little strength like

LOWLINESS

'With all lowliness and meekness, with longsuffering, forbearing one another in love' (Ephesians 4:2).

'Let nothing be done through strife or vainglory; but in lowliness of mind let each esteem other better than themselves. Look not every man on his own things, but every man also on the things of others. Let this mind be in you, which was also in Christ Jesus' (Philippians 2:3-5).

'Ye call me Master and Lord: and ye say well; for so I am' (John 13:13).

'And there was also a strife among them, which of them should be accounted the greatest. And he said unto them, The kings of the Gentiles exercise lordship over them; and they that exercise authority upon them are called benefactors. But ye shall not be so: but he that is greatest among you, let him be as the younger; and he that is chief, as he that doth serve' (Luke 22:24-26).

MEEKNESS

'With all lowliness and meekness, with longsuffering, forbearing one another in love' (*Ephesians 4:2*).

'Take my yoke upon you, and learn of me; for I am meek and lowly in heart: and ye shall find rest unto your souls' (*Matthew 11:29*).

'Put on therefore, as the elect of God, holy and beloved, bowels of mercies, kindness, humbleness of mind, meekness, longsuffering, forbearing one another, and forgiving one another, if any man have a quarrel against any: even as Christ forgave you, so also do ye' (*Colossians 3:12-13*).

'To speak evil of no man, to be no brawlers, but gentle, shewing all meekness unto all men' (*Titus 3:2*).

LONGSUFFERING

'With all lowliness and meekness, with longsuffering, forbearing one another in love' (Ephesians 4:2).

'Charity suffereth long, and is kind; charity envieth not; charity vaunteth not itself, is not puffed up, Doth not behave itself unseemly, seeketh not her own, is not easily provoked, thinketh no evil; Rejoiceth not in iniquity, but rejoiceth in the truth' (1 Corinthians 13:4-6).

'Giving no offence in anything, that the ministry be not blamed: But in all things approving ourselves as the ministers of God, in much patience, in affliction, necessities, distresses, stripes, imprisonment, tumult, labor, watch, fasting; By pureness, by knowledge, by longsuffering, by kindness, by the Holy Ghost, by love unfeigned, By the word of truth, by the power of God, by the armor of righteousness on the right hand and on the left, By honor and dishonor, by evil report and good report: as deceivers, and yet true; As unknown, and yet well known; as dying, and, behold, we live; as chastened, and not killed; As sorrowful, yet alway rejoicing; as poor, yet making many rich; as having nothing, and yet possessing all things' (2 Corinthians 6:3-10).

He can boldly discuss this with the Corinthians because of his devotion to them. Furthermore, he wrote,

'O ye Corinthians, our mouth is open unto you, our heart is enlarged. Ye are not straitened in us, but ye are straitened in your own bowels. Now for a recompence in the same, (I speak as unto my children,) be ye also enlarged. Be ye not unequally yoked together with unbelievers: for what fellowship hath righteousness with unrighteousness? And what communion hath light with darkness? And what concord hath Christ with Belial? Or what part hath he that believeth with an infidel? And what agreement hath the temple of God with idols? For ye are the temple of the living God; as God hath said, I will dwell in them, and walk in them; and I will be their God, and they shall be my people' (2 Corinthians 6:1-16).

FORBEARANCE

'With all lowliness and meekness, with longsuffering, forbearing one another in love... And be ye kind one to another, tenderhearted, forgiving one another, even as God for Christ's sake hath forgiven you' (Ephesians 4:2, 32).

'Forbearing one another, and forgiving one another, if any man has a quarrel against any: even as Christ forgave you, so also do ye' (Colossians 3:13).

LOVE

'With all lowliness and meekness, with longsuffering, forbearing one another in love' (_Ephesians 4:2_).

'Be ye therefore followers of God, as dear children. And walk in love, as Christ also hath loved us, and hath given himself for us an offering and a sacrifice to God for a sweetsmelling savor' (_Ephesians 5:1-2_).

'We love him, because he first loved us. If a man say, I love God, and hateth his brother, he is a liar: for he that loveth not his brother whom he hath seen, how can he love God whom he hath not seen? And this commandment have we from him, That he who loveth God love his brother also' (_1 John 4:19-21_).

UNITY

'Endeavouring to keep the unity of the Spirit in the bond of peace' (Ephesians 4:3).

'Neither pray I for these alone, but for them also which shall believe on me through their word; That they all may be one; as thou, Father, art in me, and I in thee, that they also may be one in us: that the world may believe that thou hast sent me. And the glory which thou gavest me I have given them; that they may be one, even as we are one: I in them, and thou in me, that they may be made perfect in one; and that the world may know that thou hast sent me, and hast loved them, as thou hast loved me' (John 17:20-23).

'For as the body is one, and hath many members, and all the members of that one body, being many, are one body: so also is Christ. For by one Spirit are we all baptized into one body, whether we be Jews or Gentiles, whether we be bond or free; and have been all made to drink into one Spirit. For the body is not one member, but many. If the foot shall say, Because I am not the hand, I am not of the body; is it therefore not of the body? And if the ear shall say, Because I am not the eye, I am not of the body; is it

therefore not of the body? If the whole body were an eye, where were the hearing? If the whole were hearing, where were the smelling? But now hath God set the members every one of them in the body, as it hath pleased him' (<u>1 Corinthians 12:12-18</u>).

'That there should be no schism in the body; but that the members should have the same care one for another' (<u>1 Corinthians 12:25</u>).

PEACE WITH ONE ANOTHER

'Endeavouring to keep the unity of the Spirit in the bond of peace' (Ephesians 4:3).

'Follow peace with all men, and holiness, without which no man shall see the Lord' (Hebrews 12:14).

'And the servant of the Lord must not strive; but be gentle unto all men, apt to teach, patient' (2 Timothy 2:24).

'Recompense to no man evil for evil. Provide things honest in the sight of all men. If it be possible, as much as lieth in you, live peaceably with all men' (Romans 12:17-18).

Bearing one another's burden

'Bear ye one another's burdens, and so fulfil the law of Christ' (Galatians 6:2).

Hospitality one to another

'Use hospitality one to another without grudging' (1Peter 4:9).

Greeting one another

'Greet ye one another with a kiss of charity. Peace be with you all that are in Christ Jesus. Amen' (1Peter 5:14).

'Salute one another with an holy kiss. The churches of Christ salute you' (*Romans 16:16*).

Comforting one another

'Wherefore comfort one another with these words' (*1Thessalonians 4:18*).

Considering one another

'And let us consider one another to provoke unto love and to good works' (*Hebrew 10:24*).

Edifying one another

'Let us therefore follow after the things which make for peace, and things wherewith one may edify another' (*Romans 14:19*).

'Wherefore comfort yourselves together, and edify one another, even as also ye do' (*1Thessalonians 5:11*).

Exhorting one another

'And I myself also am persuaded of you, my brethren, that ye also are full of goodness, filled with all knowledge, able also to admonish one another' (<u>Romans 15:14</u>).

'Let the word of Christ dwell in you richly in all wisdom; teaching and admonishing one another in psalms and hymns and spiritual songs, singing with grace in your hearts to the Lord' (<u>Colossians 3:16</u>).

Ministering one to another

'As every man hath received the gift, even so minister the same one to another, as good stewards of the manifold grace of God' (<u>1Peter 4:10</u>).

Preferring one another

'Be kindly affectioned one to another with brotherly love; in honour preferring one another' (<u>Romans 12:10</u>).

Praying one for another

'Confess your faults one to another, and pray one for another, that ye may be healed. The effectual fervent prayer of a righteous man availeth much' (<u>James 5:16</u>).

Submitting one to another

'Likewise, ye younger, submit yourselves unto the elder. Yea, all of you be subject one to another, and be clothed with humility: for God resisteth the proud, and giveth grace to the humble' (<u>1Peter 5:5</u>).

'Submitting yourselves one to another in the fear of God' (<u>Ephesians 5:21</u>).

Teaching one another

'Let the word of Christ dwell in you richly in all wisdom; teaching and admonishing one another in psalms and hymns and spiritual songs, singing with grace in your hearts to the Lord' (<u>Colossians 3:16</u>).

Forbearing one another

'Forbearing one another, and forgiving one another, if any man have a quarrel against any: even as Christ forgave you, so also do ye' (<u>Colossians 3:13</u>).

'And be ye kind one to another, tenderhearted, forgiving one another, even as God for Christ's sake hath forgiven you' (<u>Ephesians 4:32</u>).

Forgiving one another

'Forbearing one another, and forgiving one another, if any man have a quarrel against any: even as Christ forgave you, so also do ye' (<u>Colossians 3:13</u>).

'And be ye kind one to another, tenderhearted, forgiving one another, even as God for Christ's sake hath forgiven you' (<u>Ephesians 4:32</u>).

The church in Philadelphia was taught about supplication before service

'First, I thank my God through Jesus Christ for you all, that your faith is spoken of throughout the whole world. For God is my witness, whom I serve with my spirit in the gospel of his Son, that without ceasing I make mention of you always in my prayers; Making request, if by any means now at length I might have a prosperous journey by the will of God to come unto you' (<u>Romans 1:8-10</u>).

'For this cause I bow my knees unto the Father of our Lord Jesus Christ, [15] Of whom the whole family in heaven and earth is named, That he would grant you, according to the riches of his glory, to be strengthened with might by his Spirit in the inner man; That Christ may dwell in your hearts by faith; that ye, being rooted and grounded in love, May be able to comprehend with all saints what is the breadth, and length, and depth, and height; And to know the love of Christ, which passeth knowledge, that ye might be filled with all the fullness of God' (Ephesians 3:14-19).

'For God is my record, how greatly I long after you all in the bowels of Jesus Christ. And this I pray, that your love may abound yet more and more in knowledge and in all judgment; That ye may approve things that are excellent; that ye may be sincere and without offence till the day of Christ; Being filled with the fruits of righteousness, which are by Jesus Christ, unto the glory and praise of God' (Philippians 1:8-11).

'We give thanks to God and the Father of our Lord Jesus Christ, praying always for you, Since we heard of your faith in Christ Jesus, and of the love which ye have to all the saints, For the hope which is laid up for you in heaven,

whereof ye heard before in the word of the truth of the gospel; Which is come unto you, as it is in all the world; and bringeth forth fruit, as it doth also in you, since the day ye heard of it, and knew the grace of God in truth: As ye also learned of Epaphras our dear fellowservant, who is for you a faithful minister of Christ; Who also declared unto us your love in the Spirit' (Colossians 1:3-8).

He prays again for their growth in grace

'For this cause we also, since the day we heard it, do not cease to pray for you, and to desire that ye might be filled with the knowledge of his will in all wisdom and spiritual understanding; That ye might walk worthy of the Lord unto all pleasing, being fruitful in every good work, and increasing in the knowledge of God; Strengthened with all might, according to his glorious power, unto all patience and longsuffering with joyfulness; Giving thanks unto the Father, which hath made us meet to be partakers of the inheritance of the saints in light' (Colossians 1:3-8).

'We give thanks to God always for you all, making mention of you in our prayers; Remembering without ceasing your work of faith, and labour of love, and

patience of hope in our Lord Jesus Christ, in the sight of God and our Father; Knowing, brethren beloved, your election of God' (1Thessalonians 1:2-4).

Service beyond self

'For God is my witness, whom I serve with my spirit in the gospel of his Son, that without ceasing I make mention of you always in my prayers; Making request, if by any means now at length I might have a prosperous journey by the will of God to come unto you' (Romans 1:9-10).

'That I may come unto you with joy by the will of God, and may with you be refreshed' (Romans 1:15-32).

'I delight to do thy will, O my God: yea, thy law is within my heart' (Psalm 40:8).

'Cause me to hear thy lovingkindness in the morning; for in thee do I trust: cause me to know the way wherein I should walk; for I lift up my soul unto thee' (Psalm 143:8).

'Go to now, ye that say, Today or tomorrow we will go into such a city, and continue there a year, and buy and sell, and get gain: Whereas ye know not what shall be on the morrow. For what is your life? It is even a vapor that

appeareth for a little time, and then vanisheth away. For that ye ought to say, If the Lord will, we shall live, and do this, or that' (James 4:13-15).

The ministers in Philadelphia were well informed about God's kingdom life. They let every member know that they are expected to serve God, the church and the people in the worlds, sinners. They were told that they are ambassadors for Christ on earth, representatives of God and proclaimers of good news to the lost. They were told that they are light, salts and that they should shine before men in darkness so that they will see their good works and glorify God.

The churches of our time has neglected the teaching ministry of Christ, their call to make disciples and focused on power, prosperity, faith, praise ministry and empowerment for service without Christ-like life. They have ordained retired unrepentant rich armed robbers, murderers, evil senior citizens, criminals and demonized failed civil servants. This has brought confusion, problems and all manner of deaths in the body of Christ.

Many possessed sinners who came to the church to be delivered are receiving prophecies instead of deliverance from sin and the consequences of sin. Some are told that they are having problems because God called them. With their demons, without salvation, they are now recruited into the ministry to deliver others. They are told to go to school of ministry, prayers and deliverance where they learn the principles of deliverance. The ministers in Philadelphia were well informed.

1. They were taught on edifying ministry, positives preaching, Christ-like lifestyle that promote love and unity

'And he gave some, apostles; and some, prophets; and some, evangelists; and some, pastors and teachers; For the perfecting of the saints, for the work of the ministry, for the edifying of the body of Christ: Till we all come in the unity of the faith, and of the knowledge of the Son of God, unto a perfect man, unto the measure of the stature of the fullness of Christ' (Ephesians 4:11-13).

'Let us therefore follow after the things which make for peace, and things wherewith one may edify another' (Romans 14:19).

'Now I beseech you, brethren, by the name of our Lord Jesus Christ, that ye all speak the same thing, and that there be no divisions among you; but that ye be perfectly joined together in the same mind and in the same judgment' (1 Corinthians 1:10).

'I have planted, Apollos watered; but God gave the increase' (1 Corinthians 3:6).

'The one preach Christ of contention, not sincerely, supposing to add affliction to my bonds' (Philippians 1:16).

2. They were taught to do all things without pride, give credit to God and to others for progress and success instead of claiming it for themselves

'Let nothing be done through strife or vainglory; but in lowliness of mind let each esteem other better than themselves' (Philippians 2:3).

3. They were instructed against partiality, tribalism, but to give privileges and positions to those who meet scriptural qualifications

    'My brethren, have not the faith of our Lord Jesus Christ, the Lord of glory, with respect of persons' (James 2:1).

    'I charge thee before God, and the Lord Jesus Christ, and the elect angels, that thou observe these things without preferring one before another, doing nothing by partiality' (1Timothy 5:21).

    'For they that have used the office of a deacon well purchase to themselves a good degree, and great boldness in the faith which is in Christ Jesus' (1Timothy 3:13).

4. The leaders were taught to live in harmony among them

    'Thy watchmen shall lift up the voice; with the voice together shall they sing: for they shall see eye to eye, when the LORD shall bring again Zion' (Isaiah 52:8).

'But Moses' hands were heavy; and they took a stone, and put it under him, and he sat thereon; and Aaron and Hur stayed up his hands, the one on the one side, and the other on the other side; and his hands were steady until the going down of the sun' (Exodus 17:12).

5. They were taught to identify and support the mission work, village evangelism and to be committed to the same goal

'So all the men of Israel were gathered against the city, knit together as one man' (Judge 20:11).

'So built we the wall; and all the wall was joined together unto the half thereof: for the people had a mind to work' (Nehemiah 4:6).

'And it came to pass from that time forth, that the half of my servants wrought in the work, and the other half of them held both the spears, the shields, and the bows, and the habergeons; and the rulers were behind all the house of Judah. They which builded on the wall, and they that bare burdens, with those that laded, everyone with one of

his hands wrought in the work, and with the other hand held a weapon' (Nehemiah 4:16-17).

6. The pastors, ministers are to be examples to members, sinners and must manifest love, forgiveness, compassion and purity of life

'Sanctify them through thy truth: thy word is truth. As thou hast sent me into the world, even so have I also sent them into the world. And for their sakes I sanctify myself, that they also might be sanctified through the truth. Neither pray I for these alone, but for them also which shall believe on me through their word; That they all may be one; as thou, Father, art in me, and I in thee, that they also may be one in us: that the world may believe that thou hast sent me. And the glory which thou gavest me I have given them; that they may be one, even as we are one: I in them, and thou in me, that they may be made perfect in one; and that the world may know that thou hast sent me, and hast loved them, as thou hast loved me' (John 17:17-23).

7. They are to preach to sinners and get them saved, saved members to be sanctified and to be filled with the Spirit

'And be not drunk with wine, wherein is excess; but be filled with the Spirit; Speaking to yourselves in psalms and hymns and spiritual songs, singing and making melody in your heart to the Lord; Giving thanks always for all things unto God and the Father in the name of our Lord Jesus Christ; Submitting yourselves one to another in the fear of God' (Ephesians 5:18-21).

8. They are to continue in faith and encourage other saints to continue in the saint's fellowship

'Then they that gladly received his word were baptized: and the same day there were added unto them about three thousand souls. And they continued steadfastly in the apostles' doctrine and fellowship, and in breaking of bread, and in prayers. And fear came upon every soul: and many wonders and signs were done by the apostles. And all that believed were together, and had all things common; And sold their possessions and goods, and parted them to all men, as every man had need. And they,

continuing daily with one accord in the temple, and breaking bread from house to house, did eat their meat with gladness and singleness of heart, Praising God, and having favour with all the people. And the Lord added to the church daily such as should be saved' (Acts 2:41-47).

9. To love, forgive and to recognize that none essential differences must not be allowed to hinder relationship or love for each other

'New commandment I give unto you, That ye love one another; as I have loved you, that ye also love one another. By this shall all men know that ye are my disciples, if ye have love one to another' (John 13:34-35).

10. They must be humble and to recognize the place of others in the ministry

'Let nothing be done through strife or vainglory; but in lowliness of mind let each esteem other better than themselves' (Philippians 2:3).

'But now hath God set the members every one of them in the body, as it hath pleased him. And if they were all one member, where were the body? But now are they many members, yet but one body. And the eye cannot say unto the hand, I have no need of thee: nor again the head to the feet, I have no need of you. Nay, much more those members of the body, which seem to be more feeble, are necessary: And those members of the body, which we think to be less honorable, upon these we bestow more abundant honor; and our uncomely parts have more abundant comeliness. For our comely parts have no need: but God hath tempered the body together, having given more abundant honor to that part which lacked: That there should be no schism in the body; but that the members should have the same care one for another' (1Corinthians 12:18-25).

11. They must respect, obey leadership, speak, act and minister in co-operation, not in evil competition, hate speech, conspiring against any

'That ye be not slothful, but followers of them who through faith and patience inherit the promises' (Hebrews 6:12).

That ye be not slothful, but followers of them who through faith and patience inherit the promises

'Render therefore to all their dues: tribute to whom tribute is due; custom to whom custom; fear to whom fear; honor to whom honor' (Romans 13:7).

'Remember them which have the rule over you, who have spoken unto you the word of God: whose faith follow, considering the end of their conversation' (Hebrews 13:7).

'For I say, through the grace given unto me, to every man that is among you, not to think of himself more highly than he ought to think; but to think soberly, according as God hath dealt to every man the measure of faith. For as we have many members in one body, and all members have not the same office: So we, being many, are one body in Christ, and every one members one of another. Having then gifts differing according to the grace that is given to

us, whether prophecy, let us prophesy according to the proportion of faith; Or ministry, let us wait on our ministering: or he that teacheth, on teaching; Or he that exhorteth, on exhortation: he that giveth, let him do it with simplicity; he that ruleth, with diligence; he that sheweth mercy, with cheerfulness. Let love be without dissimulation. Abhor that which is evil; cleave to that which is good. Be kindly affectioned one to another with brotherly love; in honor preferring one another' (Romans 12:3-10).

Though the church in Philadelphia had not entered into the realm of the Spirit, baptism of the Holy Ghost and the gifts of the Holy Ghost, Christ praised them. He praised them for keeping, obeying, standing for and defending His words as well as not denying His name. They stood by all that the name of Christ stands for in the face of all opposition.

Christ commended them for being loyal, faithful and their commitment to Christ. They did not commercialize their little strength, divert it, bury it or ignore it to look for occult power. They used it very well, valued it so much, fought every enemy, and got victory with their little strength.

The devil knows that what you have as a born again, God's minister is bigger than all his power put together. That is why he is attacking you so that you can come to him for an exchange. He knows that the initial power, strength you received at your salvation is a priceless treasure, more valuable, powerful than all his power on earth. That is why he is oppressing you, denying you of certain things, health, peace and other things to force you, influence you to come to him for an exchange.

God is watching, examining you to see whether you will bow to the devil or to Him. You must hold fast, fight a good fight, keep what you have, your faith, finish well and receive commendation from Christ, an open door that no man can close. You need to guide your faith jealously because very soon, you will be rewarded. The battle you are going through now will soon be over and Christ will give you an open door that no man will shut.

The bridegroom will soon come and only those who still have oil in their lamps shall be empowered. Nothing must be allowed to exchange your faith, if you must please Christ who laid His life down to redeem your soul. We are living in perilous times and many have turned away from the truth unto lies, fake power and evil prosperity. They no longer preach sound word of God. They now go from place to place, city to city with fake power to seduce and put more people into bondage with evil prophecies and defiled solutions. They take the grace of God for granted and turn the grace of God into lasciviousness.

With polluted anointing and empowerment from the devil, they pretend to give charity to the poor, the widows, but they are evil. Every good thing they try to do is fake, deceitful and will put people more into bondage.

They are thieves, soul traders, destiny killers with bag of money from deceived members. They pretend to do charity work, love Christ but they break His words and keep distance from God's character.

'Verily, verily, I say unto you, If a man keep my saying, he shall never see death' (John 8:51).

'And hereby we do know that we know him, if we keep his commandments' (1 John 2:3).

'Whosoever therefore shall confess me before men, him will I confess also before my Father which is in heaven' (Matthew 10:32).

They are under the judgment of death together with their ministry and their ill-gotten wealth. They are defiled in character and polluted with everything about them. You must recognize them on time, avoid them, and break every link with them. No matter what you have invested in them, their family and ministry, walk out from them while you are still spiritual alive. Break out from their altars and turn back to God for true and holy relationship. Turn your back against them, reject their calls, text messages and seek for true power and the riches of Christ and His grace.

CHAPTER THREE

OPEN DOOR FROM CHRIST

When Christ saw that the foundational pillar of the church in Philadelphia was based on the salvation gospel, He gave them open door. When He saw that they were deadly determined to obey Him at all cost without negotiation, He gave them open door. They received open door to overcome every enemy and be freed from slavery, physical pains, sufferings, infirmities and deliverance from death.

'I know thy works: behold, I have set before thee an open door, and no man can shut it: for thou hast a little strength, and hast kept my word, and hast not denied my name' (Revelation 3:8).

'But I will tarry at Ephesus until Pentecost. For a great door and effectual is opened unto me, and there are many adversaries' (1 Corinthians 16:8-9).

Open door from Christ does not respect any limit, full stop, confinement or adversaries. The lives and ministry of the brethren in Philadelphia is evidence that all things are possible and nothing is impossible. It is an evidence that a church, a person, a group, a family, a city and nation can be delivered. Open door that comes from Christ does not respect or accept partial deliverance or evil left over. There may be an adversary, adversities but they cannot close doors opened by Christ forever.

The enemy may fight, but will not win, stop you or destroy you. Christ's open door can endure forever, resist internal and external forces. Move unmovable mountains and cure incurable sickness. An open door from Christ does not negotiate with any evil force, every knee must bow. If you receive open door from Christ, your enemy may start but they will not finish. You may have problems but they will not overcome you.

The problem of the majority of Christian community is that they do not know what they have. With little strength, the church in Philadelphia overcame all the Asian demons, including Diana of Ephesus. With little strength, their initial power of salvation, they overcame the prince that once ruled the whole world (*see* Acts 19:27). But Barnabas took him, and brought him to the apostles, and declared unto them how he had seen the Lord in the way, and that he had spoken to him, and how he had preached boldly at Damascus in the name of Jesus.

You can prosper, remain prosperous, receive God's power, remain empowered and increase in power until you become powerfully powerful without weakness.

> *'The righteous also shall hold on his way, and he that hath clean hands shall be stronger and stronger'* (*Job 17:9*).

> *'And I will wait upon the LORD, that hideth his face from the house of Jacob, and I will look for him'* (*Isaiah 8:17*).

The brethren in the church at Philadelphia entered into God's righteousness at salvation, refused to come out of that power, exchange that power, misuse that power, despise that power, toil with that power or corrupt that power. They hold on the way of that power, refused to be diverted by all forces and maintained relationship with the owner of that power to the day of their reward. They refuse to allow any defilement, hand pollutions to defile their hands.

When God saw how they used their little strength, He empowered them to be strong and stronger. They waited for God's time, God's time of visitation, God's plan and valued God's way of deliverance more than the deliverance that come from the devil.

'Furthermore, when I came to Troas to preach Christ's gospel, and a door was opened unto me of the Lord' (2 Corinthians 2:12).

'Withal praying also for us, that God would open unto us a door of utterance, to speak the mystery of Christ, for which I am also in bonds: That I may make it manifest, as I ought to speak' (Colossians 4:3-4).

Satan attacked them with arrows of delays, pains and used all manner of evil devices to take away the little strength they had but they resisted all his devices. When Christ opens a door for you, that single door will lead you to all manner of blessings, good things and overthrow your enemies. You will receive the door of utterance, power to say the right thing at the right time and nobody will say a better one. If you receive door of utterance, you will speak and every demon will not only hear, but they will obey.

In times of deliverance, whatever you utter will stand. Kings, governors, heathen rulers and world leaders will hear and obey. Door of utterance can penetrate into dark rooms of satanic kingdom and expose their secrets, destroy their plans and set captives free. Door of utterance from Christ is so powerful and more powerful than the most powerful enemy on earth.

Door of utterance from Christ can pierce into the ocean, sun, moon, stars and into bottomless pit and paralyze every evil power. It can set every captive free and disengage committed monitoring evil force in a moment of time. Instead of looking for fake power, occult power and satanic help, why don't you ask for open door for utterance? It can enter into the heart, soul, spirit, joints, marrow faster than medical surgical knives, drugs and the air.

No creature can stop the move of divine utterance. Evil magnet cannot magnet divine utterance. No hook from anywhere, cord or thorns from evil forces can prevent divine utterance from divine intentions. No appeal, supplications or covenant can persuade divine utterance from action. Soft words, violent speeches, evil utterances and curses from any evil force cannot stop divine utterance from movement.

It is easier, possible to stop a moving train, flight or ship in the sea on high speed but it is not near possible to stop divine utterance. No power among the creature, in heaven and earth can bring divine utterance into slavery or persuade Him to suspend action.

Nobody or power in the whole universe can play with divine utterance or bind Him for a moment. You cannot delay divine utterance, make a banquet for Him or block Him with iron bars. No weapon of destruction, spears can stand in the battlefield at the appearance of divine utterance. Every champion among champions of all the forces of darkness withdraws and forgets battle at the appearance of divine utterance.

The hope of experts, the best of the bests in the kingdom of darkness becomes vanity and drop down their weapons at the manifestation of divine utterance. They are cast down in submission at His sight. No power retains their power or remain fierce or dare stir Him up or stand to put up a challenge before divine utterance.

Nobody, wise or foolish among the creature has discovered how to win divine utterance in battle. Divine utterance is God Himself and is full of divine mercy. Old ministers, young ministers should go for divine utterance because He has all the mysteries yet to be exposed.

'Peter therefore was kept in prison: but prayer was made without ceasing of the church unto God for him. And when Herod would have brought him forth, the same night Peter was sleeping between two soldiers, bound with two chains: and the keepers before the door kept the prison. And, behold, the angel of the Lord came upon him, and a light shined in the prison: and he smote Peter on the side, and raised him up, saying, Arise up quickly. And his chains fell off from his hands. And the angel said unto him, Gird thyself, and bind on thy sandals. And so he did. And he saith unto him, Cast thy garment about thee, and follow me. And he went out, and followed him; and wist not that it was true which was done by the angel; but thought he saw a vision. When they were past the first and the second ward, they came unto the iron gate that leadeth unto the city; which opened to them of his own accord: and they went out, and passed on through one street; and forthwith the angel departed from him. And when Peter was come to himself, he said, Now I know of a surety, that the Lord hath sent his angel, and hath delivered me out of the hand of Herod, and from all the expectation of the people of the Jews' (Acts 12:5-11).

Through divine utterance, mysteries of life are exposed. It helps you to walk in wisdom, speak in wisdom, start in wisdom and end in wisdom. It was through the divine utterance of prayers that Peter was released from prison. Sometimes, believers that speak with divine utterance, pray with divine utterance may not understand what they say; it is a mystery of Christ. If you ask God to pray for you with divine utterance, all your locked up blessings can be released without protocol.

As a minister, a believer empowered with divine utterance, you can release millions of imprisoned blessings, marriages, wombs, health, business, finances and any good thing from satanic altars. No matter where you are, where your blessings are locked up, they can be released by divine utterance. Your spirit husband, wife, children and all ancestral powers may bound you with unbreakable chains and hand you over to the grave demons, if they hear divine utterance, they will release you.

'Jesus therefore again groaning in himself cometh to the grave. It was a cave, and a stone lay upon it...And when he thus had spoken, he cried with a loud voice, Lazarus, come forth...And he that was dead came forth, bound

hand and foot with grave clothes: and his face was bound
about with a napkin. Jesus saith unto them, Loose him,
and let him go' (John 11:38, 43-44).

No matter who is behind your problems, the chains of bondage all over you, if they hear divine utterance, those chains will fall off. The occult people against you, all the kingdom of darkness may take you far into satanic prison, behind iron gates, if they hear divine utterance, they will not keep you any longer. If you are where you are not supposed to be, where helpers cannot locate you to help you, if they hear divine utterance, they will let you go without battle.

'But the unbelieving Jews stirred up the Gentiles, and
made their minds evil affected against the brethren' (Acts
14:2).

No matter the lies against you, the gang ups and the entire witchcraft crusade, once they hear divine utterance, they will bow. This is the time for ministers, students of bible collages, church of Christ to pray and cry for door of utterance to speak the mystery of Christ to open for them. This is the time for individual Christians, every child of God to set time apart to pray for the opening of the door of utterance to break old time bondages.

The believers in Philadelphia maintained relationship with Christ and He opened this door for them. When this door was opened for them, no power on earth or in hell was able to shut it.

Listen to this:

It is unfortunate to tell you that even though this door was opened, many believers in Philadelphia could not pass through. Ignorance, prayerlessness and evil satisfaction prevented them. Some were still satisfied with what they had when God was beckoning on them for more.

Some pastors among them were still managing little anointing, few members and small salaries. It is disappointing for many ministers today to be satisfied with few members, few helpers, few sponsors and few millionaires in their congregation and few blessings when God is saying, you need more.

'But covet earnestly the best gifts: and yet shew I unto you a more excellent way' (*1 Corinthians 12:31*).

'If any of you lack wisdom, let him ask of God, that giveth to all men liberally, and upbraideth not; and it shall be given him' (*James 1:5*).

When the door was opened for the believers in Philadelphia, some of them were over holy, over righteous to ask for more strength, more power, more anointing, more grace and more expansion. The door for promotion, greatness and all manner of gift was opened for them but they never saw the needs to ask for more, seek and knock. They had opportunity to ask for many things but some of them asked for only one, two or even less, while some never see the need to ask.

'Two things have I required of thee; deny me them not before I die: Remove far from me vanity and lies: give me neither poverty nor riches; feed me with food convenient for me: Lest I be full, and deny thee, and say, Who is the LORD? Or lest I be poor, and steal, and take the name of my God in vain' (*Proverbs 30:7-9*).

Some people think that humility is by living in poverty, managing little things and remaining in sickness. No, the door that Christ opened for you now, is for total freedom and deliverance. The man in our text asked for neither poverty nor riches but for daily provision alone. You can ask for more and total eradication of poverty and release of abundance. You can be full with good things and yet serve God. Christ promised his followers, including you abundance life.

'For the LORD God is a sun and shield: the LORD will give grace and glory: no good thing will he withhold from them that walk uprightly' (Psalm 84:11).

You can have food to feed yourself, your family and a whole nation. Joseph did it and he never took the name of God in vain. You will serve God better with riches,

'After these things did king Ahasuerus promote Haman the son of Hammedatha the Agagite, and advanced him, and set his seat above all the princes that were with him. And all the king's servants, that were in the king's gate, bowed, and reverenced Haman: for the king had so commanded concerning him. But Mordecai bowed not, nor did him reverence. Then the king's servants, which were in the king's gate, said unto Mordecai, Why transgressest thou the king's commandment? Now it came to pass, when they spake daily unto him, and he hearkened not unto them, that they told Haman, to see whether Mordecai's matters would stand: for he had told them that he was a Jew. And when Haman saw that Mordecai bowed not, nor did him reverence, then was Haman full of wrath. And he thought scorn to lay hands on Mordecai alone; for they had shewed him the people of Mordecai: wherefore Haman sought to destroy all the Jews that were throughout the whole kingdom of Ahasuerus, even the people of Mordecai' (Esther 3:1-6).

You can serve God better with your increase, wealth and divine provisions that come from Him. It is better to live in a better house than to live in a bad house. It is better to be a house owner than to be a tenant. You can serve God more by lending to people instead of borrowing. You can serve God as a managing director more than being a servant, a cleaner or as nobody. There is nothing bad for praying for all your members, your family to become rich in Christ, millionaires in Christ Jesus or occupying the highest office in the land. It is not a mean thing, a joke to have an open door. Though there may be oppositions but they have no power to close the door, it is a permanent open door. There is an open door to God and His riches and to every capacity for the faithful and true children of God. Every opposition must be humbled and is humbled before you.

'Behold, I will make them of the synagogue of Satan, which say they are Jews, and are not, but do lie; behold, I will make them to come and worship before thy feet, and to know that I have loved thee' (Revelation 3:9).

Ministers and believers who left God's presence to seek help from the devil will be disgraced. It is a matter of time and all their affluence, pride; boasting and arrogance will be exposed and judged. All false prophet, prophetess, general overseers who are playing religion, claiming to be of God will be humbled.

All agents of the devil who pretend to be of God, who takes believers right, mock true children of God, will not go free. Anyone whose ministry, promotion, wealth and advancement came through falsehood, evil sacrifice will be humbled before true believers. Every honor, respect and their glory are temporary; they will be disgraced with time. Their entire plot against God's true servants will back fire.

'Then went Haman forth that day joyful and with a glad heart: but when Haman saw Mordecai in the king's gate, that he stood not up, nor moved for him, he was full of indignation against Mordecai. Nevertheless, Haman refrained himself: and when he came home, he sent and called for his friends, and Zeresh his wife. And Haman told them of the glory of his riches, and the multitude of his children, and all the things wherein the king had promoted him, and how he had advanced him above the princes and servants of the king. Haman said moreover, Yea, Esther the queen did let no man come in with the king unto the banquet that she had prepared but myself; and tomorrow am I invited unto her also with the king.

Yet all this availeth me nothing, so long as I see Mordecai the Jew sitting at the king's gate. Then said Zeresh his wife and all his friends unto him, Let a gallows be made of fifty cubits high, and tomorrow speak thou unto the king that Mordecai may be hanged thereon: then go thou in merrily with the king unto the banquet. And the thing pleased Haman; and he caused the gallows to be made´ (Esther 5:9-14).

Their joy, evil wishes, arrows, denial against true believers will receive due judgment. Their riches, testimonies of promotions, banquets on daily bases will cease without announcement. Traps, nets, holes, letters of demotion they prepared against God's children will be used against them. They will confess with their mouth all the evil they have done, planned and intents to do against God's children. Their wealth will be turned to the righteous and their glory will be transferred to God's children.

If you know the end of the wicked ministers that work for the devil, you will never envy them. They may have everything now, move with convoy, chains of cars, with security, live in the best house, build the biggest church in the city and have air conditioned cathedral, their end is disastrous, fake ministers will be humbled with time. They are like chaff without root or fruits and they will be unable to stand in the Day of Judgment.

Fake ministers will be troubled, restless and burdened without help. They shall be cut off and their own sword shall enter into their own heart. Their arms shall be broken and God shall laugh at them. The axe of justice shall fall upon them and their riches will melt. Their power will decay; sorrow will end their happiness and replace their joy with everlasting suffering. God is angry with ministers who enter into covenant with the devil to deceive His children. Their house will be emptied, their chair of office will be vacant and their estate will be without owner. They shall be blotted out and brought to the bed of penury.

They shall be gone like a passing cloud and forgotten as a dream. They will not see how close their destruction is. They may be having feasting days, banquets but there is no safe day for them. They are cursed and placed under God's wrath and anger every day. The only one choice they have is to repent or perish here and spend their eternity in hell fire.

But overcomers, the righteous, the faithful, holy and true shall be kept from the hours of temptation which shall come upon the world, to try them that dwell upon the earth.

'Because thou hast kept the word of my patience, I also will keep thee from the hour of temptation, which shall come upon all the world, to try them that dwell upon the earth' (Revelation 3:10).

'For God hath not appointed us to wrath, but to obtain salvation by our Lord Jesus Christ' (1 Thessalonians 5:9).

Ministers who remain holy, faithful and loyal to Christ will prosper and be happy. No matter how long, it shall be well with righteous ministers, believers who wait upon the Lord. God will pay back everything his ministers lost with interest. They will be preserved forever and God will not leave them in the hand of the wicked. They will have and enjoy everlasting satisfaction. Christ's letter to true believers, godly ministers and all members in faith in Philadelphia church is that true happiness does not come through occultism. True happiness is found in doing the things that gives God pleasure. Moreover, the eyes of the Lord, His face, ears, presence and power are engaged actively to help, to heal, sustain, support, protect and preserve all that trust God. Each part you take leads to a destination. But listen, strength, happiness, answers to prayers and long life belong to the upright. But, disappointments, sorrows, destructions and premature deaths await the ungodly. God has not appointed true believers to wrath but to obtain salvation by our Lord Jesus. Are you ready for His coming or do you still wish to continue in your wickedness?

'Behold, I come quickly: hold that fast which thou hast, that no man take thy crown' (*Revelation 3:11*).

'Be ye therefore ready also: for the Son of man cometh at an hour when ye think not' (*Luke 12:40*).

CHAPTER FOUR

READINESS FOR HIS COMING

Some of the few words in the letter to the contending believers in Philadelphia are for them to continue in faith. To hold what they have fast with all seriousness and fight to the end. Starting Christian life is important but finishing well is more important. Christ told them that what they have is only theirs if they guard it with jealousy.

'Behold, I come as a thief. Blessed is he that watcheth, and keepeth his garments, lest he walk naked, and they see his shame' (Revelation 16:15).

'Be ye also patient; stablish your hearts: for the coming of the Lord draweth nigh' (James 5:8).

Multitudes of Israelites were saved, redeemed and delivered from sin, idolatry and bondage. God brought them out by His mighty hand. But thousands of them died on their way to the Promised Land. What Christ was telling them is that:

1. **They must not go back to fornication**

    'But fornication, and all uncleanness, or covetousness, let it not be once named among you, as becometh saints' (<u>Ephesians 5:3</u>).

    'For it seemed good to the Holy Ghost, and to us, to lay upon you no greater burden than these necessary things; that ye abstain from meats offered to idols, and from blood, and from things strangled, and from fornication: from which if ye keep yourselves, ye shall do well. Fare ye well' (<u>Acts 15:28-29</u>).

    'Mortify therefore your members which are upon the earth; fornication, uncleanness, inordinate affection, evil concupiscence, and covetousness, which is idolatry' (<u>Colossians 3:5</u>).

2. **They must not go back to uncleanness**

    'For a dream cometh through the multitude of business; and a fool's voice is known by multitude of words' (<u>Ephesians 5:3</u>).

'*And changed the glory of the uncorruptible God into an image made like to corruptible man, and to birds, and fourfooted beasts, and creeping things. Wherefore God also gave them up to uncleanness through the lusts of their own hearts, to dishonor their own bodies between themselves*' (Romans 1:23-24).

'*What fruit had ye then in those things whereof ye are now ashamed? for the end of those things is death*' (Romans 6:21).

'*For God hath not called us unto uncleanness, but unto holiness*' (1Thessalonians 4:7).

3. **They must not go back to covetousness**

'*But fornication, and all uncleanness, or covetousness, let it not be once named among you, as becometh saints*' (Ephesians 5:3).

'*Mortify therefore your members which are upon the earth; fornication, uncleanness, inordinate affection, evil concupiscence, and covetousness, which is idolatry*' (Colossians 3:5).

'Thou shalt not covet thy neighbor's house, thou shalt not covet thy neighbor's wife, nor his manservant, nor his maidservant, nor his ox, nor his ass, nor any thing that is thy neighbor's' (Exodus 20:17).

'And they come unto thee as the people cometh, and they sit before thee as my people, and they hear thy words, but they will not do them: for with their mouth they shew much love, but their heart goeth after their covetousness' (Ezekiel 33:31).

'And he said unto them, Take heed, and beware of covetousness: for a man's life consisteth not in the abundance of the things which he possesseth' (Luke 12:15).

4.   They must not go back to filthiness

'Neither filthiness, nor foolish talking, nor jesting, which are not convenient: but rather giving of thanks' (Ephesians 5:4).

'Wherefore lay apart all filthiness and superfluity of naughtiness, and receive with meekness the engrafted word, which is able to save your souls' (James 1:21).

'But chiefly them that walk after the flesh in the lust of uncleanness, and despise government. Presumptuous are they, selfwilled, they are not afraid to speak evil of dignities' (2 Peter 2:10).

'The fool hath said in his heart, There is no God. Corrupt are they, and have done abominable iniquity: there is none that doeth good. God looked down from heaven upon the children of men, to see if there were any that did understand, that did seek God. Every one of them is gone back: they are altogether become filthy; there is none that doeth good, no, not one. Have the workers of iniquity no knowledge? Who eat up my people as they eat bread: they have not called upon God' (Psalm 53:1-4).

5. They must not go back to foolish talking

'Neither filthiness, nor foolish talking, nor jesting, which are not convenient: but rather giving of thanks' (Ephesians 5:4).

'If any man among you seem to be religious, and bridleth not his tongue, but deceiveth his own heart, this man's religion is vain. Pure religion and undefiled before God

and the Father is this, To visit the fatherless and widows in their affliction, and to keep himself unspotted from the world' (James 1:26-27).

'In the multitude of words there wanteth not sin: but he that refraineth his lips is wise' (Proverbs 10:19).

'For he that will love life, and see good days, let him refrain his tongue from evil, and his lips that they speak no guile' (1Peter 3:10).

6. They must not go back to jesting

'Neither filthiness, nor foolish talking, nor jesting, which are not convenient: but rather giving of thanks' (Ephesians 5:4).

'As a mad man who casteth firebrands, arrows, and death, So is the man that deceiveth his neighbor, and saith, Am not I in sport?' (Proverbs 26:18).

Though many people, many churches in many cities has deteriorated, backslidden, went into cultism, false doctrines, the church in Philadelphia were warned not to copy their lifestyle. They were told to hold what they have fast. They needed to know that all workers of iniquity are excluded from Christ's kingdom

'For this ye know, that no whoremonger, nor unclean person, nor covetous man, who is an idolater, hath any inheritance in the kingdom of Christ and of God' (Ephesians 5:5).

'For I say unto you, That except your righteousness shall exceed the righteousness of the scribes and Pharisees, ye shall in no case enter into the kingdom of heaven' (Matthew 5:20).

'Know ye not that your body is the temple of the Holy Ghost which is in you, which ye have of God, and ye are not your own?' (1Corinthians 6:9).

'And there shall in no wise enter into it anything that defileth, neither whatsoever worketh abomination, or maketh a lie: but they which are written in the Lamb's book of life' (Revelation 21:27).

They needed to know that God's wrath is on all the children of disobedient

> *'Let no man deceive you with vain words: for because of these things cometh the wrath of God upon the children of disobedience' (Ephesians 5:6).*

> *'For the wrath of God is revealed from heaven against all ungodliness and unrighteousness of men, who hold the truth in unrighteousness' (Romans 1:18).*

> *'But unto them that are contentious, and do not obey the truth, but obey unrighteousness, indignation and wrath' (Romans 1:18).*

Christ in His letter was telling them to keep what they have, to walk in light

> *'Be not ye therefore partakers with them. For ye were sometimes darkness, but now are ye light in the Lord: walk as children of light: (For the fruit of the Spirit is in all goodness and righteousness and truth;) Proving what is acceptable unto the Lord. And have no fellowship with*

the unfruitful works of darkness, but rather reprove them. For it is a shame even to speak of those things which are done of them in secret. But all things that are reproved are made manifest by the light: for whatsoever doth make manifest is light. Wherefore he saith, Awake thou that sleepest, and arise from the dead, and Christ shall give thee light' (Ephesians 5:7-14).

Christ told them in His letter to continue in holiness, to remain conquerors, more than conquerors over the world, the flesh and the devil. To watch and examine their relationship with God, to prove that their names are still in the book of life and they are still overcomers.

They must have:

a) **Inner victory and freedom**

'There remaineth therefore a rest to the people of God' (Hebrew 4:9).

'That he might sanctify and cleanse it with the washing of water by the word, That he might present it to himself a glorious church, not having spot, or wrinkle, or any such

thing; but that it should be holy and without blemish' (*Ephesians 5:26-27*).

'If the Son therefore shall make you free, ye shall be free indeed' (*John 8:36*).

b. They must be in unity with other believers

'For both he that sanctifieth and they who are sanctified are all of one: for which cause he is not ashamed to call them brethren' (*Hebrews 2:11*).

'Neither pray I for these alone, but for them also which shall believe on me through their word; That they all may be one; as thou, Father, art in me, and I in thee, that they also may be one in us: that the world may believe that thou hast sent me. And the glory which thou gavest me I have given them; that they may be one, even as we are one: I in them, and thou in me, that they may be made perfect in one; and that the world may know that thou hast sent me, and hast loved them, as thou hast loved me' (*John 17:20-23*).

'Only let your conversation be as it becometh the gospel of Christ: that whether I come and see you, or else be absent,

I may hear of your affairs, that ye stand fast in one spirit, with one mind striving together for the faith of the gospel' (Philippians 1:27).

'Behold, how good and how pleasant it is for brethren to dwell together in unity! It is like the precious ointment upon the head, that ran down upon the beard, even Aaron's beard: that went down to the skirts of his garments; As the dew of Hermon, and as the dew that descended upon the mountains of Zion: for there the LORD commanded the blessing, even life for evermore' (Psalm 133:1-3).

c. They must have perfect love

'And the LORD thy God will circumcise thine heart, and the heart of thy seed, to love the LORD thy God with all thine heart, and with all thy soul, that thou mayest live' (Deuteronomy 30:6).

'Jesus said unto him, Thou shalt love the Lord thy God with all thy heart, and with all thy soul, and with all thy mind' (Matthew 22:37).

'This is my commandment, That ye love one another, as I have loved you. Greater love hath no man than this, that a man lay down his life for his friends' (John 15:12-13).

d. They must have inner and outward holiness

'Blessed are they which do hunger and thirst after righteousness: for they shall be filled... Blessed are the pure in heart: for they shall see God' (Matthew 5:6, 8).

'That he would grant unto us, that we being delivered out of the hand of our enemies might serve him without fear, In holiness and righteousness before him, all the days of our life' (Luke 1:74-75).

'That they may teach the young women to be sober, to love their husbands, to love their children' (Titus 2:14).

'For a good tree bringeth not forth corrupt fruit; neither doth a corrupt tree bring forth good fruit. For every tree is known by his own fruit. For of thorns men do not gather figs, nor of a bramble bush gather they grapes' (Luke 6:43-44).

e. They must keep their motives pure and right

'Let this mind be in you, which was also in Christ Jesus' (<u>Philippians 2:5</u>).

'For to me to live is Christ, and to die is gain' (<u>Philippians 1:21</u>).

'For do I now persuade men, or God? or do I seek to please men? For if I yet pleased men, I should not be the servant of Christ' (<u>Galatians 1:10</u>).

'I receive not honor from men' (<u>John 5:41</u>).

Jesus' word, His letter was pointing to them the way to follow to get to the end and to partake in His kingdom's final reward. Their lives must be characterized by submission to God, to His word, self-abasement, self-denial, separation, and love and longsuffering. They must be free from partial obedience. Their obedience to God, His word, the ministry and leadership must be complete. The letter was pointing to the end, continually in faith, steadfast in service and obedience.

To achieve the above:

- They must serve in simplicity and sincerity

'He that findeth his life shall lose it: and he that loseth his life for my sake shall find it. He that receiveth you receiveth me, and he that receiveth me receiveth him that sent me. He that receiveth a prophet in the name of a prophet shall receive a prophet's reward; and he that receiveth a righteous man in the name of a righteous man shall receive a righteous man's reward. And whosoever shall give to drink unto one of these little ones a cup of cold water only in the name of a disciple, verily I say unto you, he shall in no wise lose his reward' (<u>Matthew 10:39-42</u>).

'When the Son of man shall come in his glory, and all the holy angels with him, then shall he sit upon the throne of his glory: And before him shall be gathered all nations: and he shall separate them one from another, as a shepherd divideth his sheep from the goats: And he shall set the sheep on his right hand, but the goats on the left. Then shall the King say unto them on his right hand, Come, ye blessed of my Father, inherit the kingdom prepared for you from the foundation of the world: For I was an hungred, and ye gave me meat: I was thirsty, and ye gave me drink: I was a stranger, and ye took me in: Naked, and ye clothed me: I was sick, and ye visited me: I

was in prison, and ye came unto me. Then shall the righteous answer him, saying, Lord, when saw we thee an hungred, and fed thee? Or thirsty, and gave thee drink? When saw we thee a stranger, and took thee in? Or naked, and clothed thee? Or when saw we thee sick, or in prison, and came unto thee? And the King shall answer and say unto them, Verily I say unto you, Inasmuch as ye have done it unto one of the least of these my brethren, ye have done it unto me. Then shall he say also unto them on the left hand, Depart from me, ye cursed, into everlasting fire, prepared for the devil and his angels: For I was an hungred, and ye gave me no meat: I was thirsty, and ye gave me no drink: I was a stranger, and ye took me not in: naked, and ye clothed me not: sick, and in prison, and ye visited me not. Then shall they also answer him, saying, Lord, when saw we thee an hungred, or athirst, or a stranger, or naked, or sick, or in prison, and did not minister unto thee? Then shall he answer them, saying, Verily I say unto you, Inasmuch as ye did it not to one of the least of these, ye did it not to me. And these shall go away into everlasting punishment: but the righteous into life eternal' (Matthew 25:31-46).

'He riseth from supper, and laid aside his garments; and took a towel, and girded himself' (John 13:4).

'Then cometh He to Simon Peter: and Peter saith unto him, Lord, dost thou wash my feet?' (John 13:6).

'Or he that exhorteth, on exhortation: he that giveth, let him do it with simplicity; he that ruleth, with diligence; he that sheweth mercy, with cheerfulness. Let love be without dissimulation. Abhor that which is evil; cleave to that which is good' (Roman 12:8-9).

- **They must serve selfless and with self-abasement**

'He riseth from supper, and laid aside his garments; and took a towel, and girded himself. After that he poureth water into a bason, and began to wash the disciples' feet, and to wipe them with the towel wherewith he was girded' (John 13:4-5).

'Let nothing be done through strife or vainglory; but in lowliness of mind let each esteem other better than themselves. Look not every man on his own things, but every man also on the things of others. Let this mind be in you, which was also in Christ Jesus: Who, being in the form of God, thought it not robbery to be equal with God:

But made himself of no reputation, and took upon him the form of a servant, and was made in the likeness of men: And being found in fashion as a man, he humbled himself, and became obedient unto death, even the death of the cross' (Philippians 2:3-8).

'Serving the Lord with all humility of mind, and with many tears, and temptations, which befell me by the lying in wait of the Jews' (Acts 20:19).

'For I say, through the grace given unto me, to every man that is among you, not to think of himself more highly than he ought to think; but to think soberly, according as God hath dealt to every man the measure of faith' (Romans 12:3).

'Be of the same mind one toward another. Mind not high things, but condescend to men of low estate. Be not wise in your own conceits' (Romans 12:16).

'He hath shewed thee, O man, what is good; and what doth the LORD require of thee, but to do justly, and to love mercy, and to walk humbly with thy God?' (Micah 6:8).

'But ye shall not be so: but he that is greatest among you, let him be as the younger; and he that is chief, as he that doth serve' (<u>Luke 22:26</u>).

'Humble yourselves in the sight of the Lord, and he shall lift you up' (<u>James 4:10</u>).

- **They must serve with seriousness and sensitivity**

  'He riseth from supper, and laid aside his garments; and took a towel, and girded himself. After that he poureth water into a bason, and began to wash the disciples' feet, and to wipe them with the towel wherewith he was girded' (<u>John 13:4-5</u>).

  'And above all things have fervent charity among yourselves: for charity shall cover the multitude of sins. [9] Use hospitality one to another without grudging. [10] As every man hath received the gift, even so minister the same one to another, as good stewards of the manifold grace of God' (<u>1 Peter 4:8-10</u>).

  'Confess your faults one to another, and pray one for another, that ye may be healed. The effectual fervent prayer of a righteous man availeth much' (<u>James 5:16</u>).

'Seeing ye have purified your souls in obeying the truth through the Spirit unto unfeigned love of the brethren, see that ye love one another with a pure heart fervently' (1 Peter 1:22).

- **They must serve with sacrifice and satisfaction**

  'Greater love hath no man than this, that a man lay down his life for his friends' (John 15:13).

  'And walk in love, as Christ also hath loved us, and hath given himself for us an offering and a sacrifice to God for a sweetsmelling savour' (Ephesians 5:2).

  'Hereby perceive we the love of God, because he laid down his life for us: and we ought to lay down our lives for the brethren' (1John 3:16).

- **They must serve with succor and supply**

  'And when the Syrians of Damascus came to succor Hadadezer king of Zobah, David slew of the Syrians two and twenty thousand men' (2 Samuel 8:5).

'And they answered the king, The man that consumed us,

and that devised against us that we should be destroyed

from remaining in any of the coasts of Israel, Let seven

men of his sons be delivered unto us, and we will hang

them up unto the LORD in Gibeah of Saul, whom the

LORD did choose. And the king said, I will give them. But

the king spared Mephibosheth, the son of Jonathan the

son of Saul, because of the LORD'S oath that was between

them, between David and Jonathan the son of Saul. But

the king took the two sons of Rizpah the daughter of Aiah,

whom she bare unto Saul, Armoni and Mephibosheth;

and the five sons of Michal the daughter of Saul, whom

she brought up for Adriel the son of Barzillai the

Meholathite: And he delivered them into the hands of the

Gibeonites, and they hanged them in the hill before the

LORD: and they fell all seven together, and were put to

death in the days of harvest, in the first days, in the

beginning of barley harvest. And Rizpah the daughter of

Aiah took sackcloth, and spread it for her upon the rock,

from the beginning of harvest until water dropped upon

them out of heaven, and suffered neither the birds of the

air to rest on them by day, nor the beasts of the field by

night. And it was told David what Rizpah the daughter of

Aiah, the concubine of Saul, had done. And David went and took the bones of Saul and the bones of Jonathan his son from the men of Jabeshgilead, which had stolen them from the street of Bethshan, where the Philistines had hanged them, when the Philistines had slain Saul in Gilboa' (2 Samuel 21:5-12).

'But by an equality, that now at this time your abundance may be a supply for their want, that their abundance also may be a supply for your want: that there may be equality' (2 Corinthians 8:14).

To be rewarded at the end, to be crowned at the end, to benefit from any service you render as a minister, believers or worker, your service must be rendered in conformity with scriptural principles and precepts. There cannot be permanent victory until the believer accepts the totality of God's word as His will to be conformed to. For obedience to God's call to have its full reward, it must be prompt. Men of pure faith are men of absolute surrender to God's will, willing to obey and completely yielded to God's will. Your faith must be the right kind of faith and the scriptural kind of faith. Ministers, believers must not remain baby Christians with faith to get and not having faith to give. God is looking for mature Christians who do not only have the faith to come and receive but who also have faith to consecrate and give all

'I have shewed you all things, how that so labouring ye ought to support the weak, and to remember the words of the Lord Jesus, how he said, It is more blessed to give than to receive' (Acts 20:35).

'So being affectionately desirous of you, we were willing to have imparted unto you, not the gospel of God only, but also our own souls, because ye were dear unto us' (1Thessalonians 2:8).

'Hereby perceive we the love of God, because he laid down his life for us: and we ought to lay down our lives for the brethren. But whoso hath this world's good, and seeth his brother have need, and shutteth up his bowels of compassion from him, how dwelleth the love of God in him?' (1John 3:16-17).

'Therefore doth my Father love me, because I lay down my life, that I might take it again. No man taketh it from me, but I lay it down of myself. I have power to lay it down,

and I have power to take it again. This commandment have I received of my Father' (John 10:17-18).

'I am crucified with Christ: nevertheless I live; yet not I, but Christ liveth in me: and the life which I now live in the flesh I live by the faith of the Son of God, who loved me, and gave himself for me' (<u>Galatians 2:20</u>).

'For even hereunto were ye called: because Christ also suffered for us, leaving us an example, that ye should follow his steps' (<u>1Peter 2:21</u>).

'He that saith he abideth in him ought himself also so to walk, even as he walked' (<u>1John 2:6</u>).

To have faith in Christ is to put complete trust in Him in everything. To be secured in Christ, you must continue in following Him and obey His word. There is no security for the rebellious or the sinning believer. The foundation of security is the grace of God and the evidence of grace is continual victory over sin, over the flesh and the world

'This is the third time I am coming to you. In the mouth of two or three witnesses shall every word be established. I told you before, and foretell you, as if I were present, the second time; and being absent now I write to them which heretofore have sinned, and to all other, that, if I come again, I will not spare' (2 Corinthians 13:1).

'And the LORD said unto Moses, Whosoever hath sinned against me, him will I blot out of my book' (Exodus 32:33).

'Remember therefore how thou hast received and heard, and hold fast, and repent. If therefore thou shalt not watch, I will come on thee as a thief, and thou shalt not know what hour I will come upon thee. Thou hast a few names even in Sardis which have not defiled their garments; and they shall walk with me in white: for they are worthy. He that overcometh, the same shall be clothed in white raiment; and I will not blot out his name out of the book of life, but I will confess his name before my Father, and before his angels' (Revelation 3:3-5).

By completely relying on God and closely following the word of God, the weakest believer can be victorious over all temptation. The purpose of heart to be true to the word and to be obedient to God at all cost will go a long way to prepare you for victory. The consciousness of God's presence will help you to watch your actions wherever you are to be steadfast. We are to do everything with the mind that Christ can come or death can take place without announcement.

To avoid being taking unawares or unprepared for His coming, you are commanded to watch and be ready. In Christ's letter to the church in Philadelphia, He told them to be patient, to establish their hearts because His coming will not be long. He counseled them to hold fast what they have, to use their little strength, their talents, gifts, and occupy until He come. He advised them to live holy, keep His commandments without spot and to remain spotless to the day of His appearing. He told them to abide in Him so that they will have confidence that when He comes, they will not be put to shame. Apart from His second coming and the rapture, death can come before the above. We must get ready, be holy on daily basis in case death comes anytime, we will be able to make it to heaven

> 'Be ye also patient; stablish your hearts: for the coming of the Lord draweth nigh. Grudge not one against another,

brethren, lest ye be condemned: behold, the judge standeth before the door' (James 5:8).

'And he called his ten servants, and delivered them ten pounds, and said unto them, Occupy till I come' (Luke 19:13).

'That thou keep this commandment without spot, unrebukeable, until the appearing of our Lord Jesus Christ' (1 Timothy 6:14).

'And now, little children, abide in him; that, when he shall appear, we may have confidence, and not be ashamed before him at his coming' (1 John 2:28).

'In those days was Hezekiah sick unto death. And the prophet Isaiah the son of Amoz came to him, and said unto him, Thussaith the LORD, Set thine house in order; for thou shalt die, and not live' (2 Kings 20:1).

'Then shall the kingdom of heaven be likened unto ten virgins, which took their lamps, and went forth to meet the bridegroom. And five of them were wise, and five were foolish. They that were foolish took their lamps, and took no oil with them: But the wise took oil in their vessels with their lamps. While the bridegroom tarried, they all slumbered and slept. And at midnight there was a cry

made, Behold, the bridegroom cometh; go ye out to meet him. Then all those virgins arose, and trimmed their lamps. And the foolish said unto the wise, Give us of your oil; for our lamps are gone out. But the wise answered, saying, Not so; lest there be not enough for us and you: but go ye rather to them that sell, and buy for yourselves. And while they went to buy, the bridegroom came; and they that were ready went in with him to the marriage: and the door was shut. Afterward came also the other virgins, saying, Lord, Lord, open to us. But he answered and said, Verily I say unto you, I know you not. Watch therefore, for ye know neither the day nor the hour wherein the Son of man cometh' (<u>Matthew 25:1-13</u>).

'Let us be glad and rejoice, and give honor to him: for the marriage of the Lamb is come, and his wife hath made herself ready. And to her was granted that she should be arrayed in fine linen, clean and white: for the fine linen is the righteousness of saints. And he saith unto me, Write, Blessed are they which are called unto the marriage supper of the Lamb. And he saith unto me, These are the true sayings of God' (<u>Revelation 19:7-9</u>).

'And he called his ten servants, and delivered them ten pounds, and said unto them, Occupy till I come' (<u>Luke 19:13</u>).

To occupy till He comes means being involved in evangelistic efforts to save souls, be involved in evangelistic efforts in city liberations, crusades and other Christian's programs must be done to win souls. After every program, there must be period of preservation of soul won for Christ.

The continued labor consists of:

VISITATION

'And he shall set the sheep on his right hand, but the goats on the left. Then shall the King say unto them on his right hand, Come, ye blessed of my Father, inherit the kingdom prepared for you from the foundation of the world: For I was an hungred, and ye gave me meat: I was thirsty, and ye gave me drink: I was a stranger, and ye took me in: Naked, and ye clothed me: I was sick, and ye visited me: I was in prison, and ye came unto me. Then shall the righteous answer him, saying, Lord, when saw we thee an hungred, and fed thee? Or thirsty, and gave thee drink? When saw we thee a stranger, and took thee in? Or naked, and clothed thee? Or when saw we thee sick, or in prison, and came unto thee? And the King shall answer and say unto them, Verily I say unto you, Inasmuch as ye have done it unto one of the least of these my brethren, ye have done it unto me' (Matthew 25:35-40).

'Pure religion and undefiled before God and the Father is this, To visit the fatherless and widows in their affliction, and to keep himself unspotted from the world' (James 1:27).

'For I long to see you, that I may impart unto you some spiritual gift, to the end ye may be established' (Romans 1:11).

INVITATION

'I was glad when they said unto me, Let us go into the house of the LORD' (*Psalm 122:1*).

'We took sweet counsel together, and walked unto the house of God in company' (*Psalm 55:14*).

'Lo, then would I wander far off, and remain in the wilderness. Selah' (*Psalm 55:7*).

'And the Spirit and the bride say, Come. And let him that heareth say, Come. And let him that is athirst come. And whosoever will, let him take the water of life freely' (*Revelation 22:17*).

INFORMATION

'Then Jesus turned, and saw them following, and saith unto them, What seek ye? They said unto him, Rabbi, (which is to say, being interpreted, Master,) where dwellest thou? He saith unto them, Come and see. They came and saw where he dwelt, and abode with him that day: for it was about the tenth hour' (John 1:38-39).

'Now when Jesus was born in Bethlehem of Judaea in the days of Herod the king, behold, there came wise men from the east to Jerusalem, Saying, Where is he that is born King of the Jews? For we have seen his star in the east, and are come to worship him' (Matthew 2:1-2).

'And they said unto him, In Bethlehem of Judaea: for thus it is written by the prophet, And thou Bethlehem, in the land of Juda, art not the least among the princes of Juda: for out of thee shall come a Governor, that shall rule my people Israel' (Matthew 2:5-6).

'Let us hold fast the profession of our faith without wavering; (for he is faithful that promised;) And let us consider one another to provoke unto love and to good works: Not forsaking the assembling of ourselves together, as the manner of some is; but exhorting one another: and *so much the more, as ye see the day approaching'*

(Hebrews 10:23-25).

PERSUASION

'Philip findeth Nathanael, and saith unto him, We have found him, of whom Moses in the law, and the prophets, did write, Jesus of Nazareth, the son of Joseph. And Nathanael said unto him, Can there any good thing come out of Nazareth? Philip saith unto him, Come and see' (John 1:45-46).

'But sanctify the Lord God in your hearts: and be ready always to give an answer to every man that asketh you a reason of the hope that is in you with meekness and fear' (1Peter 3:15).

'And when Saul was come to Jerusalem, he assayed to join himself to the disciples: but they were all afraid of him, and believed not that he was a disciple. But Barnabas took him, and brought him to the apostles, and declared unto them how he had seen the Lord in the way, and that he had spoken to him, and how he had preached boldly at Damascus in the name of Jesus. And he was with them coming in and going out at Jerusalem' (Acts 9:26-28).

PRESERVATION

'I have manifested thy name unto the men which thou gavest me out of the world: thine they were, and thou gavest them me; and they have kept thy word. Now they have known that all things whatsoever thou hast given me are of thee. For I have given unto them the words which thou gavest me; and they have received them, and have known surely that I came out from thee, and they have believed that thou didst send me. I pray for them: I pray not for the world, but for them which thou hast given me; for they are thine. And all mine are thine, and thine are mine; and I am glorified in them. And now I am no more in the world, but these are in the world, and I come to thee. Holy Father, keep through thine own name those whom thou hast given me, that they may be one, as we are. While I was with them in the world, I kept them in thy name: those that thou gavest me I have kept, and none of them is lost, but the son of perdition; that the scripture might be fulfilled' (John 17:6-12).

'In the end of the Sabbath, as it began to dawn toward the first day of the week, came Mary Magdalene and the other

Mary to see the sepulchre. And, behold, there was a great earthquake: for the angel of the Lord descended from heaven, and came and rolled back the stone from the door, and sat upon it. His countenance was like lightning, and his raiment white as snow: And for fear of him the keepers did shake, and became as dead men. And the angel answered and said unto the women, Fear not ye: for I know that ye seek Jesus, which was crucified. He is not here: for he is risen, as he said. Come, see the place where the Lord lay. And go quickly, and tell his disciples that he is risen from the dead; and, behold, he goeth before you into Galilee; there shall ye see him: lo, I have told you' (<u>Matthew 28:1-7</u>).

'And, behold, two of them went that same day to a village called Emmaus, which was from Jerusalem about threescore furlongs. And they talked together of all these things which had happened. And it came to pass, that, while they communed together and reasoned, Jesus himself drew near, and went with them. But their eyes were holden that they should not know him. And he said unto them, What manner of communications are these that ye have one to another, as ye walk, and are sad? And the one of them, whose name was Cleopas, answering said

unto him, Art thou only a stranger in Jerusalem, and hast not known the things which are come to pass there in these days? And he said unto them, What things? And they said unto him, Concerning Jesus of Nazareth, which was a prophet mighty in deed and word before God and all the people: And how the chief priests and our rulers delivered him to be condemned to death, and have crucified him. But we trusted that it had been he which should have redeemed Israel: and beside all this, today is the third day since these things were done. Yea, and certain women also of our company made us astonished, which were early at the sepulchre; And when they found not his body, they came, saying, that they had also seen a vision of angels, which said that he was alive. And certain of them which were with us went to the sepulchre, and found it even so as the women had said: but him they saw not. Then he said unto them, O fools, and slow of heart to believe all that the prophets have spoken: Ought not Christ to have suffered these things, and to enter into his glory? And beginning at Moses and all the prophets, he expounded unto them in all the scriptures the things concerning himself. And they drew nigh unto the village, whither they went: and he made as though he would have gone further.

But they constrained him, saying, Abide with us: for it is toward evening, and the day is far spent. And he went in to tarry with them. And it came to pass, as he sat at meat with them, he took bread, and blessed it, and brake, and gave to them. And their eyes were opened, and they knew him; and he vanished out of their sight. And they said one to another, Did not our heart burn within us, while he talked with us by the way, and while he opened to us the scriptures? And they rose up the same hour, and returned to Jerusalem, and found the eleven gathered together, and them that were with them, Saying, The Lord is risen indeed, and hath appeared to Simon. And they told what things were done in the way, and how he was known of them in breaking of bread. And as they thus spake, Jesus himself stood in the midst of them, and saith unto them, Peace be unto you' (Luke 24:13-36).

'After these things Jesus shewed himself again to the disciples at the sea of Tiberias; and on this wise shewed he himself. There were together Simon Peter, and Thomas called Didymus, and Nathanael of Cana in Galilee, and the sons of Zebedee, and two other of his disciples. Simon Peter saith unto them, I go a fishing. They say unto him, We also go with thee. They went forth, and entered into a

ship immediately; and that night they caught nothing. But when the morning was now come, Jesus stood on the shore: but the disciples knew not that it was Jesus. Then Jesus saith unto them, Children, have ye any meat? They answered him, No' (John 21:1-5).

1. After deliverance

'And the LORD spake unto Moses and Aaron in the land of Egypt, saying, This month shall be unto you the beginning of months: it shall be the first month of the year to you. Speak ye unto all the congregation of Israel, saying, In the tenth day of this month they shall take to them every man a lamb, according to the house of their fathers, a lamb for an house: And if the household be too little for the lamb, let him and his neighbour next unto his house take it according to the number of the souls; every man according to his eating shall make your count for the lamb. Your lamb shall be without blemish, a male of the first year: ye shall take it out from the sheep, or from the goats: And ye shall keep it up until the fourteenth day of the same month: and the whole assembly of the congregation of Israel shall kill it in the evening. And they shall take of the blood, and strike it on the two side posts

and on the upper door post of the houses, wherein they shall eat it. And they shall eat the flesh in that night, roast with fire, and unleavened bread; and with bitter herbs they shall eat it. Eat not of it raw, nor sodden at all with water, but roast with fire; his head with his legs, and with the purtenance thereof. And ye shall let nothing of it remain until the morning; and that which remaineth of it until the morning ye shall burn with fire. And thus shall ye eat it; with your loins girded, your shoes on your feet, and your staff in your hand; and ye shall eat it in haste: it is the LORD'S passover. For I will pass through the land of Egypt this night, and will smite all the firstborn in the land of Egypt, both man and beast; and against all the gods of Egypt I will execute judgment: I am the LORD. And the blood shall be to you for a token upon the houses where ye are: and when I see the blood, I will pass over you, and the plague shall not be upon you to destroy you, when I smite the land of Egypt. And this day shall be unto you for a memorial; and ye shall keep it a feast to the LORD throughout your generations; ye shall keep it a feast by an ordinance forever' (Exodus 12:1-14).

'And the children of Israel journeyed from Rameses to Succoth, about six hundred thousand on foot that were

men, beside children. And a mixed multitude went up also with them; and flocks, and herds, even very much cattle. And they baked unleavened cakes of the dough which they brought forth out of Egypt, for it was not leavened; because they were thrust out of Egypt, and could not tarry, neither had they prepared for themselves any victual' (*Exodus 12:37-39*).

'And Moses said unto the people, Remember this day, in which ye came out from Egypt, out of the house of bondage; for by strength of hand the LORD brought you out from this place: there shall no leavened bread be eaten' (Exodus 13:3).

2. Deliverance candidates must be followed up.

They must be taught to depart from Egyptian lifestyles.

'And when the people saw that Moses delayed to come down out of the mount, the people gathered themselves together unto Aaron, and said unto him, Up, make us gods, which shall go before us; for as for this Moses, the man that brought us up out of the land of Egypt, we wot not what is become of him. And Aaron said unto them, Break off the golden earrings, which are in the ears of your wives, of your sons, and of your daughters, and bring them unto me. And all the people brake off the golden earrings which were in their ears, and brought them unto Aaron. And he received them at their hand, and fashioned it with a graving tool, after he had made it a molten calf: and they said, These be thy gods, O Israel, which brought thee up out of the land of Egypt. And when Aaron saw it, he built an altar before it; and Aaron made proclamation, and said, Tomorrow is a feast to the LORD. And they rose up early on the morrow, and offered burnt offerings, and brought peace offerings; and the people sat down to eat and to drink, and rose up to play. And the LORD said unto Moses, Go, get thee down; for thy people, which thou broughtest out of the land of Egypt, have corrupted themselves: They have turned aside quickly out of the way which I commanded them: they *have made them a molten calf, and have worshipped it, and have sacrificed thereunto, and said, These be thy gods, O Israel, which have brought thee up out of the land of Egypt. And the LORD said unto Moses, I have seen this people, and, behold, it is a stiffnecked people: Now therefore let me alone, that my wrath may wax hot against them, and that I may consume them: and I will make of thee a great nation' (Exodus 32:1-10).*

'And it came to pass, as soon as he came nigh unto the camp, that he saw the calf, and the dancing: and Moses' anger waxed hot, and he cast the tables out of his hands, and brake them beneath the mount. And he took the calf which they had made, and burnt it in the fire, and ground it to powder, and strawedit upon the water, and made the children of Israel drink of it. And Moses said unto Aaron, What did this people unto thee, that thou hast brought so great a sin upon them? And Aaron said, Let not the anger of my lord wax hot: thou knowest the people, that they are set on mischief. For they said unto me, Make us gods, which shall go before us: for as for this Moses, the man that brought us up out of the land of Egypt, we wot not what is become of him' (Exodus 19-23).

3. The redeemed Israelites need constant encouragement, instruction, intercessions, protection from demonic visits.

> 'When the unclean spirit is gone out of a man, he walketh through dry places, seeking rest, and findeth none. Then he saith, I will return into my house from whence I came out; and when he is come, he findeth it empty, swept, and garnished. Then goeth he, and taketh with himself seven other spirits more wicked than himself, and they enter in and dwell there: and the last state of that man is worse than the first. Even so shall it be also unto this wicked generation' (Matthew 12:43-45).

If Moses had counted his work finished on the day Israel came out of Egypt and handed over the people to Aaron, what would be their end? If deliverance ministers only know how to cast out demons without the training on how to help the delivered candidates, they will be possessed by wicked demon. This is why many deliverance ministers and ministries are failing in ministry. After deliverance, salvation, there is always a desire for Egyptian lifestyle

'And it came to pass, when Pharaoh had let the people go, that God led them not through the way of the land of the Philistines, although that was near; for God said, Lest peradventure the people repent when they see war, and they return to Egypt' (<u>Exodus 13:17</u>).

'But he shall not multiply horses to himself, nor cause the people to return to Egypt, to the end that he should multiply horses: forasmuch as the LORD hath said unto you, Ye shall henceforth return no more that way' (<u>Deuteronomy 17:16</u>).

'And when Pharaoh drew nigh, the children of Israel lifted up their eyes, and, behold, the Egyptians marched after them; and they were sore afraid: and the children of Israel cried out unto the LORD. And they said unto Moses, Because there were no graves in Egypt, hast thou taken us away to die in the wilderness? Wherefore hast thou dealt thus with us, to carry us forth out of Egypt? Is not this the word that we did tell thee in Egypt, saying, Let us alone, that we may serve the Egyptians? For it had been better for us to serve the Egyptians, than that we should die in the wilderness. And Moses said unto the people, Fear ye not, stand still, and see the salvation of the LORD, which he will shew to you today: for the Egyptians whom ye have

seen today, ye shall see them again no more forever. The LORD shall fight for you, and ye shall hold your peace' (Exodus 14:10-14).

'And they took their journey from Elim, and all the congregation of the children of Israel came unto the wilderness of Sin, which is between Elim and Sinai, on the fifteenth day of the second month after their departing out of the land of Egypt. And the whole congregation of the children of Israel murmured against Moses and Aaron in the wilderness: And the children of Israel said unto them, Would to God we had died by the hand of the LORD in the land of Egypt, when we sat by the flesh pots, and when we did eat bread to the full; for ye have brought us forth into this wilderness, to kill this whole assembly with hunger' (Exodus 16:1-3).

'And the mixt multitude that was among them fell a lusting: and the children of Israel also wept again, and said, Who shall give us flesh to eat? We remember the fish, which we did eat in Egypt freely; the cucumbers, and the melons, and the leeks, and the onions, and the garlick: But now our soul is dried away: there is nothing at all, beside this manna, before our eyes' (Numbers 11:4-6).

'And say thou unto the people, Sanctify yourselves against tomorrow, and ye shall eat flesh: for ye have wept in the ears of the LORD, saying, Who shall give us flesh to eat? For it was well with us in Egypt: therefore, the LORD will give you flesh, and ye shall eat. Ye shall not eat one day, nor two days, nor five days, neither ten days, nor twenty days; But even a whole month, until it come out at your nostrils, and it be loathsome unto you: because that ye have despised the LORD which is among you, and have wept before him, saying, Why came we forth out of Egypt?' (Numbers 11:18-20).

'And all the congregation lifted up their voice, and cried; and the people wept that night. And all the children of Israel murmured against Moses and against Aaron: and the whole congregation said unto them, Would God that we had died in the land of Egypt! Or would God we had died in this wilderness! And wherefore hath the LORD brought us unto this land, to fall by the sword, that our wives and our children should be a prey? Were it not better for us to return into Egypt? And they said one to another, Let us make a captain, and let us return into Egypt. Then Moses and Aaron fell on their faces before all

the assembly of the congregation of the children of Israel' (<u>*Numbers 14:1-5*</u>).

'And they journeyed from mount Hor by the way of the Red sea, to compass the land of Edom: and the soul of the people was much discouraged because of the way. And the people spake against God, and against Moses, Wherefore have ye brought us up out of Egypt to die in the wilderness? For there is no bread, neither is there any water; and our soul loatheth this light bread. And the LORD sent fiery serpents among the people, and they bit the people; and much people of Israel died' (<u>*Numbers 21:4-6*</u>).

'Woe to the rebellious children, saith the LORD, that take counsel, but not of me; and that cover with a covering, but not of my spirit, that they may add sin to sin: That walk to go down into Egypt, and have not asked at my mouth; to strengthen themselves in the strength of Pharaoh, and to trust in the shadow of Egypt! Therefore shall the strength of Pharaoh be your shame, and the trust in the shadow of Egypt your confusion' (<u>*Isaiah 30:1-3*</u>).

'Woe to them that go down to Egypt for help; and stay on horses, and trust in chariots, because they are many; and in horsemen, because they are very strong; but they look

not unto the Holy One of Israel, neither seek the LORD!
Yet he also is wise, and will bring evil, and will not call
back his words: but will arise against the house of the
evildoers, and against the help of them that work iniquity.
Now the Egyptians are men, and not God; and their
horses flesh, and not spirit. When the LORD shall stretch
out his hand, both he that helpeth shall fall, and he that is
holpen shall fall down, and they all shall fail together'
(Isaiah 31:1-3).

Though Israel came out of Egypt, Egypt did not come out of Israel. Many have come out of the world but the thoughts and systems of the world need to come out of them. There is need for follow up work after deliverance and salvation. Deliverance candidates need special attention, constant watch, protection, frequent encouragements, regular study, teaching and continuous training. It is better to leave the possessed with their demons than to cast out the demons and put them into more trouble. Preachers must emphasis on the need for holy life after deliverance to avoid more trouble. A deliverance minister who commits sin, immorality with a deliverance candidate is like a man who sins with a woman in the presence of the husband or father, likewise any believer. Ministers must not turn

God's house into prostitute's brothel. Christ assured the church in Philadelphia of a reward if they endure to the end.

'Behold, I come quickly: hold that fast which thou hast, that no man take thy crown. Him that overcometh will I make a pillar in the temple of my God, and he shall go no more out: and I will write upon him the name of my God, and the name of the city of my God, which is new Jerusalem, which cometh down out of heaven from my God: and I will write upon him my new name. He that hath an ear, let him hear what the Spirit saith unto the churches' (Revelation 3:11-13).

There is reward for all who faithfully labor for the Lord. Whatever is done for the Lord will be rewarded. All sacrifice, energy, time and money spent in laboring for the Lord cannot be expended in vain because God rewards those that worship Him in truth and Spirit.

'Wherefore, my beloved brethren, be ye stedfast, unmoveable, always abounding in the work of the Lord,

forasmuch as ye know that your labour is not in vain in the Lord' (*1 Corinthians 15:58*).

Any believer who remained steadfast, unmovable, abounding in God's service will be rewarded. Believers, who obey God, keep faith, hold fast to the end, will be crowned and mightily rewarded by Christ. The overcomers who remained overcomers to the end will receive full joy. They will have access to the tree of life and will live eternally in God's presence. They will not be hurt by second death and will be empowered for leadership to rule and reign over his enemies. Overcomers will walk with white in God's presence and their names will ever be in the book of life. Overcomers have nothing to lose because even what seems to be lost will be recovered. Overcomers are marked with God's mark and they cannot be touched by evil power. Because their names are in the book of life, the devil has no power over them, how much less his agents. The case file of every overcomer is not available to the devil. They are with God and the holy angels are instructed to protect overcomers. They have access to God's throne and can approach God anytime. Overcomers are not of this world, they are just ambassadors here on earth. Their real home, mansions and inheritance are in heaven.

They shall inherit all things in heaven and on earth. Overcomers are God's heir and they have right to every good thing on earth.

> 'He that overcometh shall inherit all things; and I will be his God, and he shall be my son' (Revelation 21:7).
>
> 'And if children, then heirs; heirs of God, and joint-heirs with Christ; if so be that we suffer with him, that we may be also glorified together' (Romans 8:17).
>
> 'He that spared not his own Son, but delivered him up for us all, how shall he not with him also freely give us all things?' (Romans 8:32).

God did not make mistake when He call you His heir, He meant every letter in those words. Many children of God, overcomers are suffering today because of ignorance. It is not God's intention for any problem to prevail over the church. God wrote to us through this letter we are reading now and He called us His heir. You must not under estimate yourself again. There is much, so much waiting for the faithful overcomers. There are crowns to wear, names to bear and joys to share once we enter into God's eternal city, we are eternally secured and shall never be forgotten. As the bride bears the name of the bridegroom throughout life, the overcomers shall bear Christ's new name forever, since we belong to Him forever.

CHAPTER FIVE

SEVENTH LETTER

THE ETERNAL LIVING CHRIST

Revelation 3:14-22

This is the last of the seven churches in Asia addressed by Christ, the head and shepherd of the church. These churches actually existed at that time and they had typical and prophetic significance. The churches typify different types of churches today and they prophetically represent churches at all times, in all lands and of all church ages. The Laodicea church had no point of praise or commendation. It was, no doubt the last and the worst of all the churches.

Religion becomes a substitute for reality and Luke warmness characterized the whole church. There was not even the trace of a faithful few as in Sradis. Yet, the Lord is pictured as standing at the door of every heart, knocking and asking for entrance. What a wonderful love from the Lord who died for all, willing to save, ready to cleanse.

Christ the author, the origin of the book of Revelation is also the great counselor to all the churches. In the letter to the seven churches, He manifested the whole characteristics in its entirety. Our living eternal Christ, the great and living Savior, the first and the last, who is before the changing circumstances of life, with the final authority writes again to the seventh church in Asia.

'And unto the angel of the church of the Laodiceans write; These things saith the Amen, the faithful and true witness, the beginning of the creation of God' (Revelation 3:14).

'Jesus saith unto him, I am the way, the truth, and the life: no man cometh unto the Father, but by me' (John 14:6).

Each letter began with great attributes, characteristics and titles of Jesus Christ. "Amen" means verily, certainly or so be it, a guarantee or affirmation of the truth of a statement. He is the faithful and true witness and His words are final without question. He is the beginning and the end, the guarantor of every promise of God. Christ as the faithful witness seals every promise that God made in the scriptures. He is the beginning of the creation of God, which means, the origin, the author, the first cause of creation. He is the way, the truth and the life, the last person before God the father.

'In the beginning was the Word, and the Word was with God, and the Word was God. The same was in the beginning with God. All things were made by him; and without him was not anything made that was made. In him was life; and the life was the light of men' (John 1:1-4).

In the beginning, the word appeared and the word was with God, and the word was God. Christ is the word, is always with God, and cannot be separated from the word because He was the word and the word was God. No one can have God without the word and to reject Christ is to reject God, who is the word.

'And to know the love of Christ, which passeth knowledge, that ye might be filled with all the fullness of God' (Ephesians 3:9).

'For by him were all things created, that are in heaven, and that are in earth, visible and invisible, whether they be thrones, or dominions, or principalities, or powers: all things were created by him, and for him: And he is before all things, and by him all things consist. And he is the head of the body, the church: who is the beginning, the firstborn from the dead; that in all things he might have the preeminence' (Colossians 1:16-18).

God appeared through Christ when He created the world through Him and came to the world through Him to have fellowship with us. It was by Him that all things were created, both things in heaven, things on earth, visible and invisible. Every throne, dominion, principalities and powers, all came through Him and are under Him and for Him. Therefore, He is before all things and by Him, all things consist and come to be. He is the leader, in charge and the head of every head and nothing that had begun was begun without Him, His approval or knowledge. Christ was the first-born, the beginning and the prominence of all things. No one can ignore Him and succeed and no success is a success without Him.

'But as God is true, our word toward you was not yea and nay. For the Son of God, Jesus Christ, who was preached among you by us, even by me and Silvanus and Timotheus, was not yea and nay, but in him was yea. For all the promises of God in him are yea, and in him Amen, unto the glory of God by us' (2 Corinthians 1:18-20).

Truth starts with Christ and any church or individual that has no Christ, has no truth and any preaching that does not embrace the truth of Christ is not complete. Without Him, there will be no fulfillment of any promise because He is the Amen or so be it, a seal to every Amen.

'And unto the angel of the church of the Laodiceans write; These things saith the Amen, the faithful and true witness, the beginning of the creation of God' (Revelation 3:14).

'For I would that ye knew what great conflict I have for you, and for them at Laodicea, and for as many as have not seen my face in the flesh' (Colossians 2:1).

THE CITY OF LAODICEA

Laodicea was a rich city and the chief city in Phrygia, founded about 250 B.C. by Antiochus the second and named after his wife. It was 45 miles S.E. of Philadelphia and about 40 miles from Ephesus. It was not far from Colossi and Hierapolis. It had a very large Jewish population and also had a medical center. The Apostle Paul knew this church of Laodicea and had a great concern and love for the church. Epaphras, a servant of Christ had a great zeal for the brethren, which were in Laodicea, desiring and praying that they would be perfect and complete in all the will of God.

'For I would that ye knew what great conflict I have for you, and for them at Laodicea, and for as many as have not seen my face in the flesh; That their hearts might be comforted, being knit together in love, and unto all riches of the full assurance of understanding, to the acknowledgement of the mystery of God, and of the Father, and of Christ' (<u>Colossians 2:1-2</u>).

Paul, an apostle of Jesus Christ had previously written to them. The condition of the church moved him to pray for them, desiring that they work together in unity, divine love and to be exposed to the mystery of Christ. Epaphras fervently prayed for them and called them by name in prayer.

'Epaphras, who is one of you, a servant of Christ, saluteth you, always labouring fervently for you in prayers that ye may stand perfect and complete in all the will of God. For I bear him record, that he hath a great zeal for you, and them that are in Laodicea, and them in Hierapolis. Salute the brethren, which are in Laodicea, and Nymphas, and the church which is in his house... And when this epistle is read among you, cause that it be read also in the church of the Laodiceans; and that ye likewise read the epistle from Laodicea' (Colossians 4:12-13, 16).

The church in Laodicea was so privileged to receive and read many copies of letters from other great men of God before the present one that we are reading now. But by the time Christ address them in

Revelation chapter three through the Apostle John, about 35 years later, the church had completely become lukewarm and backslidden.

CHAPTER SIX

THE LUKEWARM CONGREGATION

What does it mean to be lukewarm, neither cold nor hot? Does it mean to be spiritually weak, feeble, tempted or of little strength? No. A bruised reed shall he not break and smoking flax shall he not quench.

> 'A bruised reed shall he not break, and smoking flax shall he not quench, till he send forth judgment unto victory' (Matthew 12:20).
>
> 'For we have not an high priest which cannot be touched with the feeling of our infirmities; but was in all points tempted like as we are, yet without sin' (Hebrews 4:15).

If these were only weak, feeble and discouraged, Christ with divine gentleness and sympathy would have encouraged and strengthen them rather than rebuking and chastising them. They were wretched, miserable, poor, blind and naked spiritually. It was a congregation of sinners and backsliders professing to be Christians. They were vile and sinful, pitiable and without the robe of righteousness. They were insincere, religious hypocrites and harder to win to Christ than cold, irreligious sinners.

'(But this spake he of the Spirit, which they that believe on him should receive: for the Holy Ghost was not yet given; because that Jesus was not yet glorified.) Many of the people therefore, when they heard this saying, said, Of a truth this is the Prophet. Others said, This is the Christ. But some said, Shall Christ come out of Galilee?' (John 7:39-41).

There are some members of the church which are nonchalant and can never be moved, no matter the move of God in their midst. They come to church but will not contribute positively or show concern. They are just on the fence, doing nothing.

'And when he was come into the temple, the chief priests and the elders of the people came unto him as he was teaching, and said, By what authority doest thou these things? And who gave thee this authority? And Jesus answered and said unto them, I also will ask you one thing, which if ye tell me, I in likewise will tell you by what authority I do these things. The baptism of John, whence was it? From heaven, or of men? And they reasoned with themselves, saying, If we shall say, From heaven; he will say unto us, Why did ye not then believe him? But if we shall say, Of men; we fear the people; for all hold John as a prophet. And they answered Jesus, and said, We cannot tell. And he said unto them, Neither tell I you by what authority I do these things. But what think ye? A certain man had two sons; and he came to the first, and said, Son, go work today in my vineyard. He answered and said, I will not: but afterward he repented, and went. And he came to the second, and said likewise. And he answered and said, I go, sir: and went not. Whether of them twain did the will of his Father? They say unto him, The first. Jesus saith unto them, Verily I say unto you, That the publicans and the harlots go into the kingdom of God before you. For John came unto you in the way of *righteousness, and ye believed him not: but the publicans and the harlots believed him: and ye, when ye had seen it, repented not afterward, that ye might believe him' (Matthew 21:23-32).*

Religious people are very knowledgeable and they know many things but they do not have relationship with God through Christ. They are faultfinders, always looking for an excuse to accuse the righteous. When I was growing up in my village, I discovered two groups of people, idol worshippers and church people. Christians and none Christians, unbelievers and believers. It was clearly defined to the understanding of even a fool. The church people, believers or Christians were collection of those who are called of God to be His children and they responded, purchased, cleansed from sin and their names written in heaven.

'Take heed therefore unto yourselves, and to all the flock, over the which the Holy Ghost hath made you overseers, to feed the church of God, which he hath purchased with his own blood' (Acts 20:28).

These sets of believers in my village are visible church Christians. They are the assembly of people who are saved and they usually come together regularly to worship and fellowship

'A new commandment I give unto you, That ye love one another; as I have loved you, that ye also love one another. By this shall all men know that ye are my disciples, if ye have love one to another' (John 13:34-35).

'Moreover if thy brother shall trespass against thee, go and tell him his fault between thee and him alone: if he shall hear thee, thou hast gained thy brother. But if he will not hear thee, then take with thee one or two more, that in the mouth of two or three witnesses every word may be established. And if he shall neglect to hear them, tell it unto the church: but if he neglect to hear the church, let him be unto thee as an heathen man and a publican' (Matthew 18:15-17).

They are saved from their sins, separated from the world; they were always in fellowship with God, and with one another. Many of them were poor but they were always happy, without worry and anxiety.

They have definite relationship with Christ. They go to church and regular bible studies, fellowships, prayers and soul winning were their hallmark. In their meeting days, bible studies, they assemble to study, learn, love, learn how to lean on God. The lives of all their members glorify God, keep bible doctrines and preach to none members. They worship God together, care for others, especially their members. They were faithful at home, at work and prayerful at all time

'And they continued stedfastly in the apostles' doctrine and fellowship, and in breaking of bread, and in prayers' (*Acts 2:42*).

'Obey them that have the rule over you, and submit yourselves: for they watch for your souls, as they that must give account, that they may do it with joy, and not with grief: for that is unprofitable for you' (*Hebrews 13:17*).

'And he gave some, apostles; and some, prophets; and some, evangelists; and some, pastors and teachers. For the perfecting of the saints, for the work of the ministry, for the edifying of the body of Christ' (*Ephesians 4:11-12*).

'Therefore they that were scattered abroad went everywhere preaching the word' (_Acts 8:4_).

'Let as many servants as are under the yoke count their own masters worthy of all honor, that the name of God and his doctrine be not blasphemed. And they that have believing masters, let them not despise them, because they are brethren; but rather do them service, because they are faithful and beloved, partakers of the benefit. These things teach and exhort' (_1 Timothy 6:1_).

'Exhort servants to be obedient unto their own masters, and to please them well in all things; not answering again; Not purloining, but shewing all good fidelity; that they may adorn the doctrine of God our Savior in all things' (_Titus 2:9-10_).

'I will therefore that men pray everywhere, lifting up holy hands, without wrath and doubting' (_1 Timothy 2:8_).

'Pray without ceasing' (_1 Thessalonians 5:17_).

THEY ARE LIKE A FAMILY

'Of whom the whole family in heaven and earth is named' (Ephesians 3:15).

LIKE A FLOCK

'Take heed therefore unto yourselves, and to all the flock, over the which the Holy Ghost hath made you overseers, to feed the church of God, which he hath purchased with his own blood' (Acts 20:28).

LIKE A VINEYARD

'For we are laborers together with God: ye are God's husbandry, ye are God's building' (1Corinthians 3:9).

AND A NATION

'But ye are a chosen generation, a royal priesthood, an holy nation, a peculiar people; that ye should shew forth the praises of him who hath called you out of darkness into his marvelous light' (1Peter 2:9).

Each member's life is determined by their spiritual experiences, love, faith, prayer life, knowledge and obedience. They do not joke with church attendance and their membership. Their members are saved from sin and they live new life

'But ye are not in the flesh, but in the Spirit, if so be that the Spirit of God dwell in you. Now if any man have not the Spirit of Christ, he is none of his' (Romans 8:9).

'Know ye not, that to whom ye yield yourselves servants to obey, his servants ye are to whom ye obey; whether of sin unto death, or of obedience unto righteousness? But God be thanked, that ye were the servants of sin, but ye have obeyed from the heart that form of doctrine, which was delivered you. Being then made free from sin, ye became

the servants of righteousness. I speak after the manner of men because of the infirmity of your flesh: for as ye have yielded your members servants to uncleanness and to iniquity unto iniquity; even so now yield your members servants to righteousness unto holiness' (<u>Romans 6:17-19</u>).

They also preach to people, none members everywhere. When they came together to fellowship, they sing and clap hands. They pray and most times, speak in tongues. Once you join their group and hear their preaching during bible study, obey and accept Christ, your parents, neighbors, school people, office, market place will know. Everywhere you go, people will quickly know that you have joined the group. Your dressing, way of life, behavior, everything about you will immediately change. Your friends, relationships with others will change.

People will call you born-again, Scripture Union (S.U), and they will begin to persecute you, call you names. Your parents, helpers will deny you of your rights, try to stop you. They called this group, Pentecostals, born again, hand clappers or people who get drunk with American drugs or charms.

The second group is churchgoers or idol worshipers. Some of them go to church and worship idol. Others go to church but they do not worship idol or physically enter into shrines. They are not outright idol worshippers, they go to church but they do not have power over sin. They are not born again, though they are baptized and given Christian names. In their church, they do not clap hands, speak in tongue or carry bible like Pentecostals those days.

While Pentecostal members, believers or born again answer Christ's call through hearing God's words, repentance, confession and forsaking of their sins, the other group answer their own call by being baptized and belonging to their church. The Pentecostal of those days get born-again; forsake sin, Satan, self to follow Christ, the Savior. They turn away from darkness to walk in the light. They enter into narrow gate to walk in the narrow way. In their bible study times, they are instructed to walk worthy of their call of salvation. Their characters change as they become members of the body of Christ

'I therefore, the prisoner of the Lord, beseech you that ye walk worthy of the vocation wherewith ye are called' (*Ephesians 4:1*).

'Then spake Jesus again unto them, saying, I am the light of the world: he that followeth me shall not walk in darkness, but shall have the light of life' (John 8:12).

'Therefore we are buried with him by baptism into death: that like as Christ was raised up from the dead by the glory of the Father, even so we also should walk in newness of life' (Romans 6:4).

'This I say therefore, and testify in the Lord, that ye henceforth walk not as other Gentiles walk, in the vanity of their mind, Having the understanding darkened, being alienated from the life of God through the ignorance that is in them, because of the blindness of their heart: Who being past feeling have given themselves over unto lasciviousness, to work all uncleanness with greediness. But ye have not so learned Christ' (Ephesians 4:17-20).

'Only let your conversation be as it becometh the gospel of Christ: that whether I come and see you, or else be absent, I may hear of your affairs, that ye stand fast in one spirit, with one mind striving together for the faith of the gospel' (Philippians 1:27).

'Brethren, be followers together of me, and mark them which walk so as ye have us for an ensample. (For many

walk, of whom I have told you often, and now tell you even weeping, that they are the enemies of the cross of Christ: Whose end is destruction, whose God is their belly, and whose glory is in their shame, who mind earthly things.)' (Philippians 3:17-19).

'That ye might walk worthy of the Lord unto all pleasing, being fruitful in every good work, and increasing in the knowledge of God' (Colossians 1:10).

They are taught that in relationship with others in the church, at home and in the society, their new life and new walk must show:

LOWLINESS

'With all lowliness and meekness, with longsuffering, forbearing one another in love' (Ephesians 4:2).

'Let nothing be done through strife or vainglory; but in lowliness of mind let each esteem other better than themselves. Look not every man on his own things, but every man also on the things of others. Let this mind be in you, which was also in Christ Jesus' (Philippians 2:3-5).

'Took branches of palm trees, and went forth to meet him, and cried, Hosanna: Blessed is the King of Israel that cometh in the name of the Lord. And Jesus, when he had found a young ass, sat thereon; as it is written, Fear not, daughter of Sion: behold, thy King cometh, sitting on an ass's colt. These things understood not his disciples at the first: but when Jesus was glorified, then remembered they that these things were written of him, and that they had done these things unto him. The people therefore that was with him when he called Lazarus out of his grave, and raised him from the dead, bare record' (John 12:13-17).

'And to offer a sacrifice according to that which is said in the law of the Lord, A pair of turtledoves, or two young pigeons. And, behold, there was a man in Jerusalem, whose name was Simeon; and the same man was just and devout, waiting for the consolation of Israel: and the Holy Ghost was upon him. And it was revealed unto him by the Holy Ghost, that he should not see death, before he had seen the Lord's Christ' (Luke 22:24-26).

MEEKNESS

'With all lowliness and meekness, with longsuffering, forbearing one another in love' (*Ephesians 4:2*).

'Take my yoke upon you, and learn of me; for I am meek and lowly in heart: and ye shall find rest unto your souls' (*Matthew 11:29*).

'Put on therefore, as the elect of God, holy and beloved, bowels of mercies, kindness, humbleness of mind, meekness, longsuffering; Forbearing one another, and forgiving one another, if any man have a quarrel against any: even as Christ forgave you, so also do ye' (*Colossians 3:12-13*).

'To speak evil of no man, to be no brawlers, but gentle, shewing all meekness unto all men' (*Titus 3:2*).

LONGSUFFERING

'With all lowliness and meekness, with longsuffering, forbearing one another in love' (Ephesians 4:2).

'Charity suffereth long, and is kind; charity envieth not; charity vaunteth not itself, is not puffed up, Doth not behave itself unseemly, seeketh not her own, is not easily provoked, thinketh no evil; Rejoiceth not in iniquity, but rejoiceth in the truth' (1 Corinthians 13:4-6).

'Giving no offence in anything, that the ministry be not blamed: But in all things approving ourselves as the ministers of God, in much patience, in afflictions, in necessities, in distresses, In stripes, in imprisonments, in tumults, in labours, in watchings, in fastings; By pureness, by knowledge, by longsuffering, by kindness, by the Holy Ghost, by love unfeigned, By the word of truth, by the power of God, by the armor of righteousness on the right hand and on the left, By honor and dishonor, by evil report and good report: as deceivers, and yet true; As unknown, and yet well known; as dying, and, behold, we live; as chastened, and not killed; As sorrowful, yet always rejoicing; as poor, yet making many rich; as having

nothing, and yet possessing all things' (2 Corinthians 6:3-
10).

He can boldly discuss this with the Corinthians because of his
devotion to them

> 'O ye Corinthians, our mouth is open unto you, our heart
> is enlarged. Ye are not straitened in us, but ye are
> straitened in your own bowels. Now for a recompence in
> the same, (I speak as unto my children,) be ye also
> enlarged. Be ye not unequally yoked together with
> unbelievers: for what fellowship hath righteousness with
> unrighteousness? And what communion hath light with
> darkness? And what concord hath Christ with Belial? Or
> what part hath he that believeth with an infidel? And
> what agreement hath the temple of God with idols? For ye
> are the temple of the living God; as God hath said, I will
> dwell in them, and walk in them; and I will be their God,
> and they shall be my people' (2 Corinthians 6:11-16).

FORBEARANCE

'With all lowliness and meekness, with longsuffering, forbearing one another in love... And be ye kind one to another, tenderhearted, forgiving one another, even as God for Christ's sake hath forgiven you' (Ephesians 4:2, 32).

'Forbearing one another, and forgiving one another, if any man have a quarrel against any: even as Christ forgave you, so also do ye' (Colossians 3:13).

LOVE

'With all lowliness and meekness, with longsuffering, forbearing one another in love' (Ephesians 4:2).

'Be ye therefore followers of God, as dear children; And walk in love, as Christ also hath loved us, and hath given himself for us an offering and a sacrifice to God for a sweetsmelling savor' (Ephesians 5:1-2).

'We love him, because he first loved us. If a man say, I love God, and hateth his brother, he is a liar: for he that loveth not his brother whom he hath seen, how can he love God whom he hath not seen? And this commandment have we from him, That he who loveth God love his brother also' (1John 4:19-21).

UNITY WITH THE CHURCH

'Blessed be the God and Father of our Lord Jesus Christ, who hath blessed us with all spiritual blessings in heavenly places in Christ' (Ephesians 4:3).

'Neither pray I for these alone, but for them also which shall believe on me through their word; That they all may be one; as thou, Father, art in me, and I in thee, that they also may be one in us: that the world may believe that thou hast sent me. And the glory which thou gavest me I have given them; that they may be one, even as we are one: I in them, and thou in me, that they may be made perfect in one; and that the world may know that thou hast sent me, and hast loved them, as thou hast loved me' (John 17:20-23).

'For as the body is one, and hath many members, and all the members of that one body, being many, are one body: so also is Christ. For by one Spirit are we all baptized into one body, whether we be Jews or Gentiles, whether we be *bond or free; and have been all made to drink into one Spirit. For the body is not one member, but many. If the foot shall say, Because I am not the hand, I am not of the body; is it therefore not of the body? And if the ear shall say, Because I am not the eye, I am not of the body; is it therefore not of the body? If the whole body were an eye, where were the hearing? If the whole were hearing, where were the smelling? But now hath God set the members every one of them in the body, as it hath pleased him'* (*1Corinthians 12:12-18*).

'That there should be no schism in the body; but that the members should have the same care one for another' (*1Corinthians 12:25*).

PEACE AMONG EACH OTHER

'Endeavouring to keep the unity of the Spirit in the bond of peace' (Ephesians 4:3).

'Follow peace with all men, and holiness, without which no man shall see the Lord' (Hebrews 12:14)

'And the servant of the Lord must not strive; but be gentle unto all men, apt to teach, patient' (2 Timothy 2:24).

'Recompense to no man evil for evil. Provide things honest in the sight of all men. If it be possible, as much as lieth in you, live peaceably with all men' (Romans 12:17-18).

I remember those days, as a young born again, new convert, immediately we finished bible study for the day, with zeal, I will go into my bible, repeat the bible quotations, read it over and over and examine my life with those bible references. Anyone I do not understand, I will go to my pastor, any leader and ask question. I make note of every bible study.

In fact, what I am telling you now is from my old bible study notebook, taught by my first Pastor Kumuyi at Gbagada Deeper Life Bible Church Gbagada, 1984. As we leave the church from every fellowship, we come out to practice it before our parents, schoolmates, neighbors, fellow believers and anyone around us. We use the bible to test ourselves to see if we are really born again. We watch how we react when others provoke us, tell lies against us.

We are happy when we suffer or denied our rights because of Christ. Those days, membership was not a mixture of wheat and tares but only those who were purchased with His own blood (*see* Acts 20:28). Church attendance and church membership are two different things. True church members hate sins; ignore sins, treats sins in the midst of sinners as if they do not exist. But people who just attend church respond to sin, play with sin and are alive to sin. Truly born-again church members are dead to sin and do not respond to the demands of the flesh. A nation does not count the dead and foreigners when citizens are being counted. Neither does a family count the dead and the fetus as part of the family. It is proper, legitimate, necessary and helpful for any church to know their members provided the dead; the foreigners and the fetus are not counted

> *'Then they that gladly received his word were baptized: and the same day there were added unto them about three thousand souls' (*Acts 2:41*).*

'Howbeit many of them which heard the word believed; and the number of the men was about five thousand' (Acts 4:4).

'And the word of God increased; and the number of the disciples multiplied in Jerusalem greatly; and a great company of the priests were obedient to the faith' (Acts 6:7).

'And when they heard it, they glorified the Lord, and said unto him, Thou seest, brother, how many thousands of Jews there are which believe; and they are all zealous of the law' (Acts 21:20).

CHAPTER SEVEN

WHAT IS REPENTANCE?

Those days, our pastors challenged us with the word of God to prove or bring forth the fruits of repentance.

- Repentance is not an abstract idea or notion that one gives a mental assent to.

- It is not a religious dogma that one believes without any practical consequence on his life and behavior.

- Repentance produces fruits and works in all those who have truly repented. Many people talk about repentance and the effect on the lives of the penitent.

- All who have repented must show the evidence of that repentance by bringing forth the fruits of repentance.

'Bring forth therefore fruits meet for repentance: And think not to say within yourselves, We have Abraham to our father: for I say unto you, that God is able of these stones to raise up children unto Abraham. And now also the axe is laid unto the root of the trees: therefore every

tree which bringeth not forth good fruit is hewn down, and cast into the fire' (Matthew 3:8-10).

- Many great evangelists, pastors, prophets and other titled ministers gather multitudes but cannot show tangible fruits of repentance of the flock.

- There are ministers, pastors who are ministering to many, pastoring many but they refused to be ministered to or pastored.

- They just learn one kingdom language, got occult power and start deceiving people. They boast of their gifts, talents, prosperity, claim to attend bible school, deliverance school, prayer school but they cannot bring forth any fruit of their acclaimed repentance.

- They exact people, tell lies with God's name, prophesy falsely to take members money. Most of them are jobless, lazy and possessed by evil spirits. Prodigal sons and daughters that refuse to repent.

- True repentance leads to a change of conduct, change of mind and must produce a change of action.

- It is not a mere change of opinion; it goes much deeper to bring real reformation of life. Repentance consists of a radical change of mind about God, sin, about self and about the world.

- Previously, sin was delighted in, but now it is hated and mourned over.

- Previously, self was esteemed, but now it is abhorred.

- Previously, you are of the world and his friendship was sought and prized, now your hearts have been diverted from the world and you regard it as your enemy.

- Repentance softens the hard soil of the soul and makes it receptive to the gospel seed.

- To repent is to confess and forsake all known sins.

'He that covereth his sins shall not prosper: but whoso confesseth and forsaketh them shall have mercy' (<u>Proverbs 28:13</u>).

- Repentance is turning away from sin, turning of heart against sin, change of heart concerning sin.

- Without true repentance, you cannot believe in Christ to be saved.

- Mental acknowledgement of Christ is not faith in Christ. The heart that clings to sin cannot truly exercise faith in Christ.

'And I will lay it waste: it shall not be pruned, nor digged; but there shall come up briers and thorns: I will also command the clouds that they rain no rain upon it. For the vineyard of the LORD of hosts is the house of Israel, and the men of Judah his pleasant plant: and he looked

for judgment, but behold oppression; for righteousness,
but behold a cry' (Isaiah 5:6-7).

- To have faith in Christ is to put your complete trust in Him for forgiveness, peace and reconciliation with God.

- When you repent and believe in Christ, you are saved. To be secured in Christ, you must continue following Christ, obeying His words.

- There is no security for the rebellious or sinning Christian.

- The foundation of security is the grace of God and the evidence of grace is continual victory over sin, the flesh and the world.

- True repentance produces always the fruits of righteousness and new life.

'I have heard of thee by the hearing of the ear: but now
mine eye seeth thee. Wherefore I abhor myself, and repent
in dust and ashes' (Job 42:5).

- If you repent truly, you discontinue from your old ways of evil word, like jokes, old use of sinful slangs and conversation, evil business tricks.

- If you remain cold and lukewarm in spiritual matters, identify yourself with the impenitent unrepentant world, you are not born again.

If you are born-again, you will abhor detestable sins like the following -

1. Pride – (Proverbs 6:16-17, 16:18-19, 21:4, Mark 7:20-23, 1Timothy 3:6, James 4:6).

2. Lying – (Proverbs 6:17, 11:1, 19:9, Ephesians 4:25, Revelation 21:8).

3. Murder – (Proverbs 6:17, Romans 1:28-32, Matthew 5:21-22, 1John 3:15).

4. Evil imaginations and plans – (Proverbs 6:18, Micah 2:1-3, Job 5:12).

5. Mischief and wickedness – (Proverbs 6:12-15, 18, Isaiah 59:1-8, Acts 13:10-11).

6. Perjury – (Proverbs 6:19, 19:5, 25:18, Exodus 23:1, Deuteronomy 19:16-21).

7. Sowing discord – (Proverbs 6:12-15, 19, 16:28, 2 Thessalonians 3:11, 1Timothy 5:13).

8. Adultery and fornication – (Proverbs 6:25-35, 7:24-27, Job 31:9-12, Mark 7:20-23, Acts 15:29, 1Corinthians 6:9-10, Revelation 2:20-23).

9. Stealing – (Ephesians 4:29, Psalms 12:3, 52:2-4, Proverbs 16:27-28, 26:22, Matthew 12:34-37).

10. Bitterness and wrath – (Ephesians 4:31, Hebrews 12:15-17, James 3:14-16).

11. Anger and clamor – (<u>Ephesians 4:31</u>, <u>Psalm 37:8</u>, <u>Proverbs 6:32</u>, <u>Mathew 5:22</u>).

12. Malice – (<u>Ephesians 4:3</u>, <u>Colossians 3:8</u>, <u>1Peter 2:1</u>).

13. Grieving the Holy Spirit – (<u>Ephesians 4:30</u>, <u>Isaiah 63:10</u>, <u>Acts 5:3, 7:51</u>).

14. Uncleanness – (<u>Ephesians 5:3</u>, <u>Romans 1:23-24</u>, <u>6:21</u>, <u>1Thessalonians 4:7</u>).

15. Covetousness – (<u>Ephesians 5:3</u>, <u>Colossians 3:5</u>, <u>Exodus 20:17</u>, <u>Ezekiel 33:31</u>, <u>Luke 12:15</u>).

16. Filthiness – (<u>Ephesians 5:4</u>, <u>James 1:21</u>, <u>2Peter 2:10</u>, <u>Psalms 53:1-4</u>).

17. Foolish talking – (<u>Ephesians 5:4</u>, <u>James 1:26-27</u>, <u>Proverbs 10:19</u>, <u>1Peter 3:10</u>).

18. Jesting – (<u>Ephesians 5:4</u>, <u>Proverbs 26:18-19</u>).

Beginning Of Church's Lukewarmness

Like I said earlier, the last group of people in my village, the idol worshippers and the churchgoers, who were not born again later joined, I mean idol worshippers and unrepentant churchgoers. The churchgoers dominated them, compelled them to join them to church. Join the zone, get baptized, and start taking Holy Communion. The youth among them literally forced their old parents, real idol worshippers to follow them to church, forced them to wed at old age and join the zone.

Once you meet up, get baptized in water, you become a member and if you die, the zonal branch will bury you, pray high-level prayers for you and assure their living members that the dead went to heaven. The priest will pray on the grave, anoint it and the deceived members will believe that he went to heaven. Heaven became very cheap and as they go to church, belonged to a particular zone, they still worshipped their idols freely. Most of their priests are in modern cult but they practice biblical idolatry. Surprisingly, the youth and women among them began to read the bible, form groups, clap hands in their groups and speak in tongues like Pentecostals. Few of them, among, the youth were ordained as priests and began to preach like Pentecostals, speak in tongues.

With time, everyone began to go to church. The church elders, senior ordained priests and bishops tried to stop them but could not. Now, everyone carry bible, preach, pray, clap hands, speak in tongues and perform miracles. There is confusion everywhere because everyone, each party, both the Pentecostals, believed that they are children of God. Everyone speak the same Christian language, praise God, God bless you, sing the same song and heal the sick.

'And Moses and Aaron went in unto Pharaoh, and they did so as the LORD had commanded: and Aaron cast down his rod before Pharaoh, and before his servants, and it became a serpent. Then Pharaoh also called the wise men and the sorcerers: now the magicians of Egypt, they also did in like manner with their enchantments. For they cast down every man his rod, and they became serpents: but Aaron's rod swallowed up their rods. And he hardened Pharaoh's heart, that he hearkened not unto them; as the LORD had said' (Exodus 7:10-13).

Moses and Aaron were in one side, with a rod while Pharaoh, his wise men, the sorcerers and magicians were in one side with their enchantment. Both produced result and made Pharaoh to harden his heart. Both parties separated and continued with what they believed, challenging themselves from time to time.

'And Moses and Aaron did so, as the LORD commanded; and he lifted up the rod, and smote the waters that were in the river, in the sight of Pharaoh, and in the sight of his servants; and all the waters that were in the river were turned to blood. And the fish that was in the river died; and the river stank, and the Egyptians could not drink of the water of the river; and there was blood throughout all the land of Egypt. And the magicians of Egypt did so with their enchantments: and Pharaoh's heart was hardened, neither did he hearken unto them; as the LORD had said' (Exodus 7:20-22).

'And the LORD spake unto Moses, Say unto Aaron, Stretch forth thine hand with thy rod over the streams, over the rivers, and over the ponds, and cause frogs to come up upon the land of Egypt. And Aaron stretched out his hand over the waters of Egypt; and the frogs came up, and covered the land of Egypt. And the magicians did so *with their enchantments, and brought up frogs upon the land of Egypt' (Exodus 8:5-7).*

'And the LORD said unto Moses, Rise up early in the morning, and stand before Pharaoh; lo, he cometh forth to the water; and say unto him, Thus saith the LORD, Let my people go, that they may serve me. Else, if thou wilt not let my people go, behold, I will send swarms of flies upon thee, and upon thy servants, and upon thy people, and into thy houses: and the houses of the Egyptians shall be full of swarms of flies, and also the ground whereon they are. And I will sever in that day the land of Goshen, in which my people dwell, that no swarms of flies shall be there; to the end thou mayest know that I am the LORD in the midst of the earth. And I will put a division between my people and thy people: tomorrow shall this sign be' (Exodus 8:20-23).

'And it came to pass on the morrow, that the evil spirit from God came upon Saul, and he prophesied in the midst of the house: and David played with his hand, as at other times: and there was a javelin in Saul's hand. And Saul cast the javelin; for he said, I will smite David even to the wall with it. And David avoided out of his presence twice' (1Samuel 18:10-11).

As I searched the scriptures, I discovered that every genuine thing that God does, Satan would try to bring along counterfeit to confuse the minds of men, deceive his followers and harden their hearts. Moses and Aaron's group, the Pentecostals, continued until God gave them victory, their opponent, confessed that power pass power.

> 'And these are the names of the sons of Levi according to their generations; Gershon, and Kohath, and Merari: and the years of the life of Levi were an hundred thirty and seven years. The sons of Gershon; Libni, and Shimi, according to their families. And the sons of Kohath; Amram, and Izhar, and Hebron, and Uzziel: and the years of the life of Kohath were an hundred thirty and three years. And the sons of Merari; Mahali and Mushi: these are the families of Levi according to their generations' (Exodus 8:16-19).

But instead of the Pentecostals of our time to continue, they compromised and left the source of their power, which is preaching, teaching and discipleship. They followed the servants of Pharaoh, the sorcerers, the magicians and continued in competition. They compromised, modified their preaching, their teaching, bowed to the pressure groups, influenced by Satan and self who judge things carnally by outward appearance only. They craved for popularity, praise of men and they backslide.

'Woe unto you, when all men shall speak well of you! For so did their fathers to the false prophets' (Luke 6:26).

Today, everyone is seeking for prophecy, no one is ready to preach, teach and tell people the truth. Once you can prophecy, tell people what they want to hear, even if you are a devil, they follow you anywhere you go. Before, ministers were likened to -

Ambassadors (Ephesians 3:20),

Servants (Philippians 1, Galatians 1:10),

Builders (1Corinthians 3:10),

Chosen Vessel (Acts 9:15, 2 Corinthians 4:7),

Stewards (1 Corinthians 4:1-2, Luke 16:1-2)

Ministers of the New Testament (1Corinthians 3:6, 4:1-2).

But today, reverse is the case, our modern ministers are small gods, occult grandmasters and if you question their actions, they will curse you. They forget that Christ in the body carried out a divinely appointed mission. He mixed up, humbled himself and revealed the love and grace of God to man. He gave up everything – position, right, glory, life to reconcile man to God. With that mission accomplished, He left the world and went to the father in heaven.

When He left, He left the church behind to carry out and continue the same mission to reveal God to man through Christ and reconcile man to God through Christ to the whole of humanity. Every member of the church is expected to do the will of God in carrying on the mission of Christ. Jesus went to individuals, preached in the cities, sent his disciples. They evangelized, edify, witness, worship, testified, taught and disciple. They practiced personal evangelism and their preaching produced conviction of sin but today, reverse is the case. The whole church has backslide, seeking for personal gain.

'The fruit of the righteous is a tree of life; and he that winneth souls is wise' (Proverbs 11:30).

Churches are no longer winning soul; they are winning people's money. The word win is a military term. To win a city is to lay siege on it and take it. It calls for skill, patience, bravery and endurance. It is also an occupational term. Like a fisherman, the soul winner, in the face of all kinds of weather and risks, applies himself to the task of skillfully bringing the sinner to Christ. Moreover, it is a matrimonial term. To win a soul to Christ is like winning a bride for the bridegroom and it takes prayer, affection, attention, sincerity, sacrifice and honest communication.

Consequences Of Backsliding Elders, Pentecostalism

- They became covetous (Genesis 13:10),

- They compromised (Genesis 13:12-13),

- They were influenced by the worldly society (Hosea 7:8-9, 1 Samuel 8:19-20, 2 Kings 17:15),

- Pride entered them (Proverbs 16:18),

- They lusted for the flesh (Nehemiah 13:26, Judges 16:14-20),

- They entered into self-indulgence (Genesis 9:1, 20-21);

- They loved money (1Timothy 6:9-10, John 13:29, Joshua 7:20-21),

- They loved the world (2 Timothy 4:10),

- They cared so much for this world (Mark 4:18-19),

- They used authority inordinately (2 Chronicles 16:9-12, 26:15-20),

- They entered into unbelief (Hebrews 3:12, 78:18-22, 2 Kings 1:2-4),

- They became prayer less (Matthew 26:40-41, 58).

- They created vacancy in the office of leadership in the church (Exodus 32:1, Judges 17:6),

- They brought bad examples in the church (Isaiah 56:10-12),

- They became immoral (1Samuel 7:12-17, 22, 8:10-21, Jeremiah 23:9-16),

- They allowed false prophecies to come into the church (Jeremiah 2:8, 10:21, 12:10, Isaiah 28:7),

- They preferred compromising preachers (Numbers 14:1-4, 2 Timothy 4:3-4, Isaiah 30:9-10),

- They desired temporary blessings above spiritual blessings (John 6:10-15, 25-35, 60, 66, Psalms 106:13-16),

- They encouraged partial obedience, unfaithfulness and insecurity (1Samuel 15:7-11, 16:14, Acts 5:1-10, Revelation 22:18-19),

- They preferred prosperity and abundance without holiness and zeal (Deuteronomy 32:5, 6, 15, Jeremiah 22:21-22, Revelation 3:14-20),

- They allowed strange preachers with false doctrines (Jeremiah 5:31, Hosea 4:6).

- The worse, they fight over positions, ordained themselves with the highest ordination in the church without God's approval.

- They also ordained unconverted women, children without experience to lead the church

> 'As for my people, children are their oppressors, and
> women rule over them. O my people, they which lead thee

*cause thee to err, and destroy the way of thy paths...
What mean ye that ye beat my people to pieces, and grind
the faces of the poor? saith the Lord GOD of hosts' (Isaiah
3:12, 15).*

*'But there was none like unto Ahab, which did sell himself
to work wickedness in the sight of the LORD, whom
Jezebel his wife stirred up' (1Kings 21:25).*

Immediately these prophetess, young boys with talents got into
leadership without much knowledge about God, his word and ways,
they conspired against the church, break away, began to prophesy.
Multitudes from the church followed them, especially youths and the
women.

*'Thus saith the LORD, Stand ye in the ways, and see, and
ask for the old paths, where is the good way, and walk
therein, and ye shall find rest for your souls. But they said,
We will not walk therein. Also I set watchmen over you,
saying, Hearken to the sound of the trumpet. But they
said, We will not hearken' (Jeremiah 6:16-17).*

The Pentecostal youths followed suit and became worse, break the congregation and took away the members.

These youths, full of strength left without permission, instruction, commission and blessings from the leaders. The leaders cursed them, prayed against them and destroyed their ministries because they took away the people that pay them tithes. The church became poor, left with few members and leaders with big tithes. God withdrew His presence from the church and they experienced unanswered prayers. They started suffering under the power of darkness causing sickness, mysterious deaths and all manner of problems.

God in His infinite mercy call those youths to stand on the truth of God's word, ask for the old paths, the good way, walk therein, find rest for their souls and break out from the curses of the elders they left but they refused. Because of their in experience, zeal without knowledge and curse from their abandoned leaders, they refused to obey God.

'But this thing commanded I them, saying, Obey my voice, and I will be your God, and ye shall be my people: and walk ye in all the ways that I have commanded you, that it may be well unto you. But they hearkened not, nor

inclined their ear, but walked in the counsels and in the
imagination of their evil heart, and went backward, and
not forward... Yet they hearkened not unto me, nor
inclined their ear, but hardened their neck: they did worse
than their fathers. Therefore thou shalt speak all these
words unto them; but they will not hearken to thee: thou
shalt also call unto them; but they will not answer thee'
(Jeremiah 7:23-24, 26-27).

God left them and they became an outcast, captive, leper, their names was removed from the book of life and God forsook them (Exodus 32:33), the wrath of God came upon them (Ezra 8:22, Job 34:26-27), God rejected them (1 Samuel 15:22-26, 1Corinthians 9:27). They became spiritually dead (1Timothy 5:14-16, Ezekiel 18:24, 26), they became exposed to demonic attacks (1Samuel 16:14, John 13:26-27, Luke 11:24-26). They became enslaved to Satan (1Timothy 5:15), their consciences were seared with a rod of iron (1Timothy 4:1, 22). Like Saul, they went and sought for help from a witch doctor and occults (1Samuel 28:6-7).

In the process of looking for solution for their problems, these youths enter into covenant with evil spirits. Some died physically while the remaining that came out alive died spiritually. They are the ones that you see around the cities pulling cloud.

Gathering the properties in the cities, building mansions, cathedrals without building lives. They drive the best cars, knows the people that matters, deceiving and being deceived. They claim to have power to see, hear, heal, prosper and deliver people but they are liars, their power is powerless and their deliverance is not delivered. They are swindlers, carnal, full of greed, pride, anger, jealousy, covetous, unfaithful and possessed with the spirit of mammon, always talking about seed sowing, money.

They are irresponsible, unfaithful in marriage without any discipline. They do not cast out demons; they transfer them, suspend their actions for a while or see problems without giving you solutions. They draw cloud; render the archbishops, bishops and old prophets in Laodicea useless without members. Their churches and remaining members are lukewarm. Laodicea church was abandoned and is the only church out of the seven churches in Asia that had no point of praise or commendation.

Religion became a substitute for reality and Luke warmness characterized the whole church, not even a trace of faithful few as in Sardis was found among them. They were all lukewarm, neither cold nor hot. They were all wretched, miserable, poor, blind and naked spiritually. They were all congregation of sinners, backsliders professing to be Christian leaders but they were vile, sinful, and pitiable, without the robe of righteousness. Most of their leaders were in cults, witchcraft groups and very insincere, religious, hypocritical and harder to win to Christ than cold, irreligious sinners.

'I know thy works, that thou art neither cold nor hot: I would thou wert cold or hot. So then because thou art lukewarm, and neither cold nor hot, I will spue thee out of my mouth. Because thou sayest, I am rich, and increased with goods, and have need of nothing; and knowest not that thou art wretched, and miserable, and poor, and blind, and naked' (Revelation 3:15-17).

Even with their condition, backslidden state, Christ wrote to them. The letter was addressed to all, the elders and the youth ministers. Christ was and still, is pictured as standing at the door of every heart, church knocking and asking for entrance.

' I counsel thee to buy of me gold tried in the fire, that thou mayest be rich; and white raiment, that thou mayest be clothed, and that the shame of thy nakedness do not appear; and anoint thine eyes with eyesalve, that thou mayest see. As many as I love, I rebuke and chasten: be zealous therefore, and repent. Behold, I stand at the door, and knock: if any man hear my voice, and open the door, I will come in to him, and will sup with him, and he with me' (Revelation 3:18-20).

Luke warmness brings shame, reproach and disgrace. It brings spiritual pollutions, decay, and all manner of poverty, uncleanness, nakedness, spiritual blindness and chastisement. Christ's counsel to the lukewarm church in Laodicea is to repent. He promises to come back to deliver them, anyone of them who will hear, open the door of his heart, church, sup with Him and be with Him.

The letter is to the whole church and individual who will respond to His request, no matter how bad you are, how wicked you are and how far you have gone away from God, you can still be delivered. If you can leave your evil way of life, dubious way of life and submit to God's deliverance program, you will be delivered, set free and restored back to God. To please God means to repent, confess and forsake all your sins and you will be forgiven.

> 'Cast away from you all your transgressions, whereby ye have transgressed; and make you a new heart and a new spirit: for why will ye die, O house of Israel?' (*Ezekiel 18:31*).

> 'Say unto them, As I live, saith the Lord GOD, I have no pleasure in the death of the wicked; but that the wicked turn from his way and live: turn ye, turn ye from your evil ways; for why will ye die, O house of Israel?' (*Ezekiel 33:11*).

You can disown your transgressions in a moment of time; receive a new heart, a new spirit and a brand new life now if you repent. God is not happy the way things are going in your life, your suffering and hardship. He is not willing or has any pleasure in your death. What God wants from you is to turn from your wicked ways, evil pursuits to avoid death. What God demands from you are not difficult, impossible or what you cannot do. He is willing and determined to help you if you want.

'And saying, Repent ye: for the kingdom of heaven is at hand' (Matthew 3:2).

'And the times of this ignorance God winked at; but now commandeth all men everywhere to repent' (Acts 17:30).

You can enter into the kingdom of heaven while you are here on earth. Part of heaven's provision can be made available to you while you are still here on earth. It can start now, if you repent with all your heart and decide to serve God only.

'Now then we are ambassadors for Christ, as though God did beseech you by us: we pray you in Christ's stead, be ye reconciled to God' (2 Corinthians 5:20).

God has decided to forget all your evil acts against Him and humankind. It is a time of your ignorance if you can repent now and forsake all your sins. He wants to empower you with true power, everlasting power, unstoppable anointing and abundant life. Not all

184 • Prayer M. Madueke

hope is lost for a repentant sinner. Though your past conducts and profession had been so disgusting and offensive, yet if you repent, seek things above, not on things on earth and open the door of your heart to receive the waiting knocking Christ, salvation and heaven will be yours.

> 'And he that overcometh, and keepeth my works unto the end, to him will I give power over the nations' (_Revelation 2:26_).

> 'To him that overcometh will I grant to sit with me in my throne, even as I also overcame, and am set down with my Father in his throne. He that hath an ear, let him hear what the Spirit saith unto the churches' (_Revelation 3:21-22_).

You need to understand that there is a battle going on against you and Christ is standing by to help you to overcome. There is a lasting crown for you if you overcome. You will start enjoying divine presence, divine defense and divine provisions. To hear other words, read other letters and fail in this very one is the worst failure. You need to be fast; open your ears hear and do what the Holy Spirit expects of you. If you need deliverance in any area of your life, that is the purpose of this letter. Christ is here, with all determination, in all His power to deliver any congregation that is ready for deliverance.

'And I saw, and behold a white horse: and he that sat on him had a bow; and a crown was given unto him: and he went forth conquering, and to conquer' (Revelation 6:2).

'And every man that striveth for the mastery is temperate in all things. Now they do it to obtain a corruptible crown; but we an incorruptible' (1 Corinthians 9:25).

'Henceforth there is laid up for me a crown of righteousness, which the Lord, the righteous judge, shall give me at that day: and not to me only, but unto all them also that love his appearing' (2 Timothy 4:8).

The power that the devil, the occult, his agents have given you may be to gather few cloud, two million people out of millions of tens in your city. He may not give you the power to gather up to 1% of the people in the city where you live in. You just gather few thousands and you are happy. You may be your church's deliverance minister, pastor or bishop of three million members.

Christ's letter says, if you overcome and keep His works unto the end, He will give you power, not to have rule over just America, one nation, but power over nations. Everything in that nation, the banks, the oil companies are yours. What are you benefitting in the occult, witchcraft group that you cannot get in nations? It is ignorance, foolishness to remain in bondage when your deliverer is just by your door knocking.

What are you looking for that Christ cannot give you or cannot do for you? This is your opportunity to get full help and full deliverance. Jesus, the man in white horse, with absolute holiness and power to set you free from your captors is standing by your door. His crown is everlasting and other powers that has crown, gives crowns, bows at His feet. Why would you seek for any crown from evil source when Christ is saying to you, come and take my crown, an everlasting crown that cannot fade away?

'Blessed is the man that endureth temptation: for when he is tried, he shall receive the crown of life, which the Lord hath promised to them that love him' (James 1:12).

'And when the chief Shepherd shall appear, ye shall receive a crown of glory that fadeth not away' (<u>1 Peter 5:4</u>).

Whatever you can do to reject what you receive from the devil, from the occult or satanic agents, do so now. The reason is that the letter you are reading now is from Christ. A line in that letter is promising you an incorruptible crown that can never fade away. This is a crown of righteousness from the righteous judge, the great Amen with everlasting seal.

'Behold, I come quickly: hold that fast which thou hast, that no man take thy crown' (<u>Revelation 3:11</u>).

'The four and twenty elders fall down before him that sat on the throne, and worship him that liveth for ever and ever, and cast their crowns before the throne, saying' (<u>Revelation 4:10</u>)

'And he said unto him, Well, thou good servant: because thou hast been faithful in a very little, have thou authority over ten cities' (<u>Luke 19:17</u>).

The devil can give you crown or crowns, promise you heaven and earth but remember, he is a liar and there is no truth in him. Christ is the truth, the way and life, His promises are yes and Amen. He has promised you in this program crown of life, you can join the overcomers today. If you love Christ, you will be happy to please Him, make Him happy and be proud of you. To love Him, you must keep His word, obey His word and be ready to pay any price to keep His commandment.

All the glory attached to whatever the devil has given you, the position and power you now enjoy is temporary. In the kingdom of darkness, whatever they promise you is not up to the glory that is attached to crown of glory that Christ will give you and has promised you. You cannot receive Christ's glory if you still keep Satan's glory. It is not possible to serve God and the devil at the same time.

Crowns are exchangeable, it is better to exchange the devil's crown, gifts, blessings, power with what God gives than to do otherwise. It is better to receive everlasting crown from the everlasting Christ than to receive a temporary crown that will bring tears into your eyes later. It is better to receive crown from the one that sits on the throne than the one that was over thrown from heaven. It is better to receive crown from Him that is worshipped and liveth forever and ever than to receive it from a failure like the devil. It is disgracing, worst to receive any crown from any person, group that is less than the devil, his agents, occult or witch doctor. What an insult to submit to the devil, his agents or any evil group.

The leaders of the church in Laodicea were struggling for position in the city and lost the church to the spirit of Luke warmness. You do not need to struggle for anything, be it power, position or any blessing. The power you have now may be just for one place, a city church branch; Christ's promise to overcomers is authority over cities. If you become an overcomer, a saint, Christ's promise is to empower you to judge the world, not just where you are now. You will have power to talk to any part of the world and they will obey you.

Do not allow the devil or one small occult you belong to keep limiting you. You have a promise to be established globally in whatever you are doing. Your business, job, profession will take you to the world, all places and advertise you beyond your location. What you have now is too small; the smallest thing to compare with what Christ wants to do in your life, if you join the overcomers. Why do you choose to deal with small matters, blessings, contract, open door, anointing and smallest problems when you have the opportunity to go worldwide, limitless and without boundary?

I counsel you; join the overcomers, the winners on the Lord's side. If you know what God have for you, you will ignore any suffering before you now, face any opposition against your becoming an overcomer and with your last strength, fight to the end. The glory before you, waiting for you to overcome is beyond explanation, more than what any occult group can offer and the whole world put together. Are you afraid of the devil; are you under his threats, or his agents and all the evil forces put together?

Listen, whatever they can do is likened to light affliction, small problem, trouble, a moment to compare to the external, everlasting, continuous and voluminous weight of glory that Christ is standing before you to give. Ignore everything, all things and press forward to be an overcomer and you will not suffer the rest of your life, here and in eternity. The overcomers will share in Christ's honor and triumph. Do you know what that offers means? It is beyond me to explain because it is better experienced than to say. The church of our time, ministers and members need deliverance that will lead to everlasting inheritance.

CHAPTER EIGHT

THE LAST DAYS

The broad outline of the book of Revelation is in this verse;

'Write the things which thou hast seen, and the things which are, and the things which shall be hereafter' (*Revelation 1:19*).

The book of Revelation has three main sections. Section one is contained in chapter one, which we have already handled. Section two is contained in chapter two and three, which we have already seen also. The next section comprises of the rest of the book, which we are about to look into now. In chapter two and three, we see the church on earth. Chapter four introduces us to the church worshipping God in heaven.

'After this I looked, and, behold, a door was opened in heaven: and the first voice which I heard was as it were of a trumpet talking with me; which said, Come up hither, *and I will shew thee things which must be hereafter. And immediately I was in the spirit: and, behold, a throne was set in heaven, and one sat on the throne. And he that sat was to look upon like a jasper and a sardine stone: and there was a rainbow round about the throne, in sight like unto an emerald. And round about the throne were four and twenty seats: and upon the seats I saw four and twenty elders sitting, clothed in white raiment; and they had on their heads crowns of gold. And out of the throne proceeded lightnings and thunderings and voices: and there were seven lamps of fire burning before the throne, which are the seven Spirits of God. And before the throne there was a sea of glass like unto crystal: and in the midst of the throne, and round about the throne, were four beasts full of eyes before and behind' (Revelation 4:1-6).*

What happens then between Revelation 3:22 and Revelation 4:1? This is the mystery

'Behold, I shew you a mystery; We shall not all sleep, but we shall all be changed, In a moment, in the twinkling of an eye, at the last trump: for the trumpet shall sound, and

the dead shall be raised incorruptible, and we shall be changed' (1Corinthians 15:51-52).

The word mystery means something which is concealed or hidden, that has to be revealed before it can be understood. No one would have understood it now except those who are taught of God. We are living in the last time, later days and the condition we are facing now in the professing or visible church at these closing days of the church center around a system of denials. There will be and there is a denial of God.

'And as it was in the days of Noah, so shall it be also in the days of the Son of man. They did eat, they drank, they married wives, they were given in marriage, until the day that Noah entered into the ark, and the flood came, and destroyed them all. Likewise also as it was in the days of Lot; they did eat, they drank, they bought, they sold, they planted, they builded; But the same day that Lot went out of Sodom it rained fire and brimstone from heaven, and destroyed them all. Even thus shall it be in the day when the Son of man is revealed' (Luke 17:26-30).

The church and the whole world are experiencing the days of Noah. The days of Noah brought the end of that age and generation. The people of that age abandoned God, denied and ignored His presence on earth. They were only concerned about self, what to eat, drink and engage themselves in. All their prayer points, energies and resources were lavished on pleasing themselves, eating, drinking and getting married. Marriage foundation, purpose and plan were destroyed. They got married, separated, divorced without considering God's law concerning marriage. They ignored the preaching of Noah concerning his revelation for the end. None was investing in the things of God. Only Noah spent his time, resources and everything building the ark of salvation. All their investment was on physical things, not spiritual. Business plans, how to buy, what to sell to make more money, plant and build occupied the whole age

> 'Traitors, heady, high-minded, lovers of pleasures more than lovers of God; Having a form of godliness, but denying the power thereof: from such turn away' (2 Timothy 3:4-5).

All over the ages like today, men became traitors, heady, high-minded, lovers of pleasures more than lovers of God. They were calling God, attending fellowship at times, but their focus was not on

God. They belong to church; places of service, but their hearts were wicked. They have the form of godliness but they lack the power of holy living, power to do good and live right. God was not involved in their eating, drinking, marriages, buying, selling and buildings.

'Now the Spirit speaketh expressly, that in the latter times some shall depart from the faith, giving heed to seducing spirits, and doctrines of devils; Speaking lies in hypocrisy; having their conscience seared with a hot iron; Forbidding to marry, and commanding to abstain from meats, which God hath created to be received with thanksgiving of them which believe and know the truth. For every creature of God is good, and nothing to be refused, if it be received with thanksgiving' (1Timothy 4:1-4).

It was an age and time of denial of faith also. Majority of people without shame left the faith they once professed concerning Christ. Others entered into relationships that were strange, covenanted with strange spirits. They were seduced to bring certain strange things, took actions against God directly. They came up with destructive doctrines, lies and hypocrisy. They abandoned God without considering the consequences until their conscience was seared with hot iron.

Some of them without enough grace entered into covenant with some organizations, religious authorities and vowed not to get married. Such doctrines of the devil affected their vow because majority of them committed abominable sexual offences. They committed lesbianism, practice gay and all manner of sexual perversion and denied their faith, messed up their vows and oath of celibacy. As a result, because of what is happening in Christendom, around us, all over the world, many have denied Christ

'Little children, it is the last time: and as ye have heard that antichrist shall come, even now are there many antichrists; whereby we know that it is the last time' (1 John 2:18).

'And every spirit that confesseth not that Jesus Christ is come in the flesh is not of God: and this is that spirit of antichrist, whereof ye have heard that it should come; and even now already is it in the world' (1 John 4:3).

'Which have forsaken the right way, and are gone astray, following the way of Balaam the son of Bosor, who loved the wages of unrighteousness' (2 Peter 2:15).

Many no longer believe that Christ's coming is a reality; they deny the second coming of Christ and all the preaching concerning that

> *'Knowing this first, that there shall come in the last days scoffers, walking after their own lusts, And saying, Where is the promise of his coming? For since the fathers fell asleep, all things continue as they were from the beginning of the creation' (2 Peter 3:3-4).*

They now mock, make jest of people that preach the coming of Christ and scoff such doctrine. They used to believe but not anymore. They are deceived and they lived their lives anyhow. They despised and deny anyone preaching sound doctrine, Christian living and authority.

> *'For the time will come when they will not endure sound doctrine; but after their own lusts shall they heap to themselves teachers, having itching ears' (2 Timothy 4:3).*
>
> *'And they shall turn away their ears from the truth, and shall be turned unto fables. But watch thou in all things,*

endure afflictions, do the work of an evangelist, make full proof of thy ministry. For I am now ready to be offered, and the time of my departure is at hand. I have fought a good fight, I have finished my course, I have kept the faith: Henceforth there is laid up for me a crown of righteousness, which the Lord, the righteous judge, shall give me at that day: and not to me only, but unto all them also that love his appearing' (2 Timothy 4:4-8).

'How that they told you there should be mockers in the last time, who should walk after their own ungodly lusts' (Jude 1:18).

As Noah and Lot ignored the mockeries of the people of their time, prepared their soul, served God and they were not disappointed, so shall it be for true Christians of our time. The imminent, soon, sudden and unannounced return of Christ is our hope and expectation.

'Watch ye therefore, and pray always, that ye may be accounted worthy to escape all these things that shall come to pass, and to stand before the Son of man' (Luke 21:36).

'So Christ was once offered to bear the sins of many; and unto them that look for him shall he appear the second time without sin unto salvation' (Hebrews 9:28).

'For our conversation is in heaven; from whence also we look for the Savior, the Lord Jesus Christ' (Philippians 3:20).

'For the grace of God that bringeth salvation hath appeared to all men, Teaching us that, denying ungodliness and worldly lusts, we should live soberly, righteously, and godly, in this present world; Looking for that blessed hope, and the glorious appearing of the great God and our Savior Jesus Christ' (Titus 2:11-13).

'Yea doubtless, and I count all things but loss for the excellency of the knowledge of Christ Jesus my Lord: for whom I have suffered the loss of all things, and do count them but dung, that I may win Christ, And be found in him, not having mine own righteousness, which is of the law, but that which is through the faith of Christ, the righteousness which is of God by faith: That I may know him, and the power of his resurrection, and the fellowship of his sufferings, being made conformable unto

his death; If by any means I might attain unto the resurrection of the dead' (Philippians 3:8-11).

'For I am now ready to be offered, and the time of my departure is at hand. I have fought a good fight, I have finished my course, I have kept the faith: Henceforth there is laid up for me a crown of righteousness, which the Lord, the righteous judge, shall give me at that day: and not to me only, but unto all them also that love his appearing' (2 Timothy 4:6-8).

CHAPTER NINE

THE MYSTERY, THE RAPTURE

Rapture is the catching up of all true believers in Christ to meet the Lord in the air. It is the time when Christ comes for the saints.

'But I would not have you to be ignorant, brethren, concerning them which are asleep, that ye sorrow not, even as others which have no hope. For if we believe that Jesus died and rose again, even so them also which sleep in Jesus will God bring with him. For this we say unto you by the word of the Lord, that we which are alive and remain unto the coming of the Lord shall not prevent them which are asleep. For the Lord himself shall descend from heaven with a shout, with the voice of the archangel, and with the trump of God: and the dead in Christ shall rise first: Then we which are alive and remain shall be caught up together with them in the clouds, to meet the Lord in the air: and so shall we ever be with the Lord. Wherefore comfort one another with these words' (1 Thessalonians 4:13-18).

It will occur at the sound of the trumpet and all that died in faith, in Christ will be raised incorruptible, changed in a moment. Death will be paralyzed and rendered impotent before everyone who died righteous and buried in the grave. At the sound of the trumpet, living believers who are in faith, at that point in time shall be caught up together to be with the Lord Jesus. It is going to be a happy re-union, an everlasting come together with the saints and Christ. At the rapture, Christ does not appear visibly to those on the earth but only comes in the air to resurrect the true saints who have died, change the living saints and catch them up to meet with Him in the air. This will all happen in the twinkling of an eye.

'For since by man came death, by man came also the resurrection of the dead' (1Corinthians 15:21).

'Behold, I shew you a mystery; We shall not all sleep, but we shall all be changed, In a moment, in the twinkling of an eye, at the last trump: for the trumpet shall sound, and the dead shall be raised incorruptible, and we shall be changed. For this corruptible must put on incorruption, and this mortal must put on immortality. So when this corruptible shall have put on incorruption, and this mortal shall have put on immortality, then shall be brought to pass the saying that is written, Death is

swallowed up in victory. O death, where is thy sting? O grave, where is thy victory? The sting of death is sin; and the strength of sin is the law. But thanks be to God, which giveth us the victory through our Lord Jesus Christ. Therefore, my beloved brethren, be ye steadfast, unmoveable, always abounding in the work of the Lord, forasmuch as ye know that your labor is not in vain in the Lord' (1Corinthians 15:51-58).

'For our conversation is in heaven; from whence also we look for the Savior, the Lord Jesus Christ. Who shall change our vile body that it may be fashioned like unto his glorious body, according to the working whereby he is able even to subdue all things unto himself' (Philippians 3:20).

'But I would not have you to be ignorant, brethren, concerning them which are asleep, that ye sorrow not, even as others which have no hope. For if we believe that Jesus died and rose again, even so them also which sleep in Jesus will God bring with him. For this we say unto you by the word of the Lord, that we which are alive and remain unto the coming of the Lord shall not prevent them which are asleep. For the Lord himself shall descend from heaven with a shout, with the voice of the archangel, and with the trump of God: and the dead in Christ shall rise first: Then

we which are alive and remain shall be caught up together with them in the clouds, to meet the Lord in the air: and so shall we ever be with the Lord' (1Thessalonians 4:13-17).

We shall be changed and caught up; transformed and translated.

'And take heed to yourselves, lest at any time your hearts be overcharged with surfeiting, and drunkenness, and cares of this life, and so that day come upon you unawares. For as a snare shall it come on all them that dwell on the face of the whole earth. Watch ye therefore, and pray always, that ye may be accounted worthy to escape all these things that shall come to pass, and to stand before the Son of man.

Every believer must take heed, be watchful all the time so that it will not take him unaware. Even right things must be done with care and moderation to avoid careless and unnecessary regret. Nothing should be done with excess to avoid being snared. The word and direct counsel from Christ to all believers is watch, pray always to escape the coming dangers. Believers, born again Christians on earth are Christ's ambassadors and ambassadors are called home before war is declared on any nation' (<u>Luke 21:34-36</u>).

'Now then we are ambassadors for Christ, as though God did beseech you by us: we pray you in Christ's stead, be ye reconciled to God' (<u>2 Corinthians 5:20</u>).

Before wrath is poured out upon this world during great tribulation, God will snatch away His *Enochs, Noahs* and *Lots*.

'And Enoch walked with God: and he was not; for God took him' (<u>Genesis 5:24</u>).

'By faith Enoch was translated that he should not see death; and was not found, because God had translated him: for before his translation he had this testimony, that he pleased God' (Hebrew 11:5).

'And it came to pass, as they still went on, and talked, that, behold, there appeared a chariot of fire, and horses of fire, and parted them both asunder; and Elijah went up by a whirlwind into heaven. And Elisha saw it, and he cried, My father, my father, the chariot of Israel, and the

horsemen thereof. And he saw him no more: and he took hold of his own clothes, and rent them in two pieces' (2 Kings 2:11).

'And when he had spoken these things, while they beheld, he was taken up; and a cloud received him out of their sight. And while they looked steadfastly toward heaven as he went up, behold, two men stood by them in white apparel; Which also said, Ye men of Galilee, why stand ye gazing up into heaven? This same Jesus, which is taken up from you into heaven, shall so come in like manner as ye have seen him go into heaven' (Acts 1:9-11).

God's purpose for the rapture:

1. To resurrect all the just and righteous people who have died (1 Thessalonians 4:13-16, 1 Corinthians 15:23, 51-58, Revelation 20:4-6).

2. To change the bodies of living saints, all who are saved by faith in Christ from mortality to immortality (1 Corinthians 15:51-58, Philippians 3:20-21, 2 Corinthians 5:1-8).

3. To take the saints out of this world before the tribulation so they can escape the tribulation (1 Thessalonians 4:13-17. Luke 21:34-36, 2 Thessalonians 2:1, 7-8, Genesis 19:12-17).

4. To take the saints to Himself (John 14:1-3, 1 Thessalonians 4:17, Ephesians 5:27, 2 Thessalonians 2:1).

5. To gather the saints together to partake of the marriage supper of the Lamb and to receive their rewards for all their labor.

'And after these things I heard a great voice of much people in heaven, saying, Alleluia; Salvation, and glory, and honor, and power, unto the Lord our God: For true and righteous are his judgments: for he hath judged the great whore, which did corrupt the earth with her fornication, and hath avenged the blood of his servants at her hand. And again they said, Alleluia. And her smoke rose up for ever and ever. And the four and twenty elders and the four beasts fell down and worshipped God that sat on the throne, saying, Amen; Alleluia. And a voice came out of the throne, saying, Praise our God, all ye his servants, and ye that fear him, both small and great. And I heard as it were the voice of a great multitude, and as the voice of many waters, and as the voice of mighty thunderings, saying, Alleluia: for the Lord God omnipotent reigneth. Let us be glad and rejoice, and give honor to him: for the marriage of the Lamb is come, and

his wife hath made herself ready. And to her was granted that she should be arrayed in fine linen, clean and white: for the fine linen is the righteousness of saints. And he saith unto me, Write, Blessed are they which are called unto the marriage supper of the Lamb. And he saith unto me, These are the true sayings of God. And I fell at his feet to worship him. And he said unto me, See thou do it not: I am thy fellow servant, and of thy brethren that have the testimony of Jesus: worship God: for the testimony of Jesus is the spirit of prophecy. And I saw heaven opened, and behold a white horse; and he that sat upon him was called Faithful and True, and in righteousness he doth judge and make war' (Revelation 19:1-11).

'We are confident, I say, and willing rather to be absent from the body, and to be present with the Lord. Wherefore we labor, that, whether present or absent, we may be accepted of him. For we must all appear before the judgment seat of Christ; that every one may receive the things done in his body, according to that he hath done, whether it be good or bad' (2 Corinthians 5:8-10).

It is important for every believer to know that the rapture can take place any moment from now. All that supposes to happen before the rapture takes place are presently happening now. The qualification to be raptured is to be saved, remain saved and maintain a holy walk in Christ at the time of the rapture or at the time of death as the case may be.

'Therefore thus will I do unto thee, O Israel: and because I will do this unto thee, prepare to meet thy God, O Israel' (Amos 4:12).

Just as Enoch and Elijah was taken up in heaven alive without sleeping or going through death, so also the saints, believers who are living at the moment of rapture will be translated to meet the Lord in the air. And just as Noah escaped the flood and Lot escaped the judgment of the fire on Sodom and Gomorrah, so the saints living then will escape the great tribulation. All believers go through persecution and tribulation.

'These things I have spoken unto you, that in me ye might have peace. In the world ye shall have tribulation: but be of good cheer; I have overcome the world' (John 16:33).

'And the hand of the Lord was with them: and a great number believed, and turned unto the Lord. Then tidings of these things came unto the ears of the church which was in Jerusalem: and they sent forth Barnabas, that he should go as far as Antioch' (Acts 14:21-22).

'And not only so, but we glory in tribulations also: knowing that tribulation worketh patience; And patience, experience; and experience, hope: And hope maketh not ashamed; because the love of God is shed abroad in our hearts by the Holy Ghost which is given unto us' (Romans 5:3-5).

'That no man should be moved by these afflictions: for yourselves know that we are appointed thereunto. For verily, when we were with you, we told you before that we should suffer tribulation; even as it came to pass, and ye know. For this cause, when I could no longer forbear, I sent to know your faith, lest by some means the tempter have tempted you, and our labor be in vain' (1 Thessalonians 3:3-5).

'But thou hast fully known my doctrine, manner of life, purpose, faith, longsuffering, charity, patience, [11] Persecutions, afflictions, which came unto me at Antioch, at Iconium, at Lystra; what persecutions I

endured: but out of them all the Lord delivered me. [12] Yea, and all that will live godly in Christ Jesus shall suffer persecution' (2 Timothy 3:10-12).

'I know thy works, and tribulation, and poverty, (but thou art rich) and I know the blasphemy of them which say they are Jews, and are not, but are the synagogue of Satan' (Revelation 2:9).

True Christians who are alive during rapture will not experience the great tribulation because they will be raptured, caught up in the air before Jacob's trouble as it is called;

'Alas! For that day is great, so that none is like it: it is even the time of Jacob's trouble; but he shall be saved out of it' (Jeremiah 30:7).

'And take heed to yourselves, lest at any time your hearts be overcharged with surfeiting, and drunkenness, and cares of this life, and so that day come upon you unawares. For as a snare shall it come on all them that dwell on the face of the whole earth. Watch ye therefore, and pray always, that ye may be accounted worthy to

escape all these things that shall come to pass, and to stand before the Son of man' (Luke 21:34-36).

If you are free from sin at the point of rapture or death, you will escape it.

'Behold, what manner of love the Father hath bestowed upon us, that we should be called the sons of God: therefore the world knoweth us not, because it knew him not. Beloved, now are we the sons of God, and it doth not yet appear what we shall be: but we know that, when he shall appear, we shall be like him; for we shall see him as he is. And every man that hath this hope in him purifieth himself, even as he is pure' (1 John 3:1-3).

'Follow peace with all men, and holiness, without which no man shall see the Lord:

If you maintain good relationship with God, have supreme love to God, you will escape the great tribulation' (Hebrews 12:14).

'But what things were gain to me, those I counted loss for Christ. Yea doubtless, and I count all things but loss for the excellency of the knowledge of Christ Jesus my Lord:

for whom I have suffered the loss of all things, and do count them but dung, that I may win Christ, And be found in him, not having mine own righteousness, which is of the law, but that which is through the faith of Christ, the righteousness which is of God by faith: That I may know him, and the power of his resurrection, and the fellowship of his sufferings, being made conformable unto his death; If by any means I might attain unto the resurrection of the dead. Not as though I had already attained, either were already perfect: but I follow after, if that I may apprehend that for which also I am apprehended of Christ Jesus. Brethren, I count not myself to have apprehended: but this one thing I do, forgetting those things which are behind, and reaching forth unto those things which are before, I press toward the mark for the prize of the high calling of God in Christ Jesus' (Philippians 3:7-14).

He further exhorts the Philippians to think and act as mature Christians.

'Let us therefore, as many as be perfect, be thus minded: and if in anything ye be otherwise minded, God shall reveal even this unto you. Nevertheless, whereto we have already attained, let us walk by the same rule, let us mind the same thing' (Philippians 3:15-16).

And to imitate him (Christ)

'Brethren, be followers together of me, and mark them which walk so as ye have us for an ensample. (For many walk, of whom I have told you often, and now tell you even weeping, that they are the enemies of the cross of Christ: Whose end is destruction, whose God is their belly, and whose glory is in their shame, who mind earthly things.) For our conversation is in heaven; from whence also we look for the Savior, the Lord Jesus Christ: Who shall change our vile body, that it may be fashioned like unto his glorious body, according to the working whereby he is able even to subdue all things unto himself' (Philippians 3:17-21).

'That the aged men be sober, grave, temperate, sound in faith, in charity, in patience. The aged women likewise, *that they be in behavior as becometh holiness, not false accusers, not given to much wine, teachers of good things; That they may teach the young women to be sober, to love their husbands, to love their children, To be discreet, chaste, keepers at home, good, obedient to their own husbands, that the word of God be not blasphemed. Young men likewise exhort to be sober minded. In all things shewing thyself a pattern of good works: in doctrine shewing uncorruptness, gravity, sincerity, Sound speech, that cannot be condemned; that he that is of the contrary part may be ashamed, having no evil thing to say of you. Exhort servants to be obedient unto their own masters, and to please them well in all things; not answering again; Not purloining, but shewing all good fidelity; that they may adorn the doctrine of God our Savior in all things. For the grace of God that bringeth salvation hath appeared to all men, Teaching us that, denying ungodliness and worldly lusts, we should live soberly, righteously, and godly, in this present world; Looking for that blessed hope, and the glorious appearing of the great God and our Savior Jesus Christ; Who gave himself for us, that he might redeem us from all iniquity, and purify unto himself a peculiar people, zealous of good works' (Titus 2:2-14).*

Doing the work of God with the eternity in view always will also qualify you for the rapture

'And the men said unto Lot, Hast thou here any besides? Son in law, and thy sons, and thy daughters, and whatsoever thou hast in the city, bring them out of this place: For we will destroy this place, because the cry of them is waxen great before the face of the LORD; and the LORD hath sent us to destroy it. And Lot went out, and spake unto his sons in law, which married his daughters, and said, Up, get you out of this place; for the LORD will destroy this city. But he seemed as one that mocked unto his sons in law. And when the morning arose, then the angels hastened Lot, saying, Arise, take thy wife, and thy two daughters, which are here; lest thou be consumed in the iniquity of the city. And while he lingered, the men laid hold upon his hand, and upon the hand of his wife, and upon the hand of his two daughters; the LORD being merciful unto him: and they brought him forth, and set* *him without the city. And it came to pass, when they had brought them forth abroad, that he said, Escape for thy life; look not behind thee, neither stay thou in all the plain; escape to the mountain, lest thou be consumed'* (<u>Genesis 19:12-17</u>).

'Say not ye, There are yet four months, and then cometh harvest? Behold, I say unto you, Lift up your eyes, and look on the fields; for they are white already to harvest. And he that reapeth receiveth wages, and gathereth fruit unto life eternal: that both he that soweth and he that reapeth may rejoice together. And herein is that saying true, One soweth, and another reapeth. I sent you to reap that whereon ye bestowed no labor: other men labored, and ye are entered into their labors' (<u>John 4:35-38</u>).

'And as Jesus passed by, he saw a man which was blind from his birth. And his disciples asked him, saying, Master, who did sin, this man, or his parents, that he was born blind? Jesus answered, Neither hath this man sinned, nor his parents: but that the works of God should be made manifest in him. I must work the works of him that sent me, while it is day: the night cometh, when no man can work' (<u>John 9:1-4</u>).

'And, behold, I come quickly; and my reward is with me, to give every man according as his work shall be. I am Alpha and Omega, the beginning and the end, the first and the last. Blessed are they that do his commandments that they may have right to the tree of life, and may enter in through the gates into the city. For without are dogs, and sorcerers, and whoremongers, and murderers, and idolaters, and whosoever loveth and maketh a lie. I Jesus have sent mine angel to testify unto you these things in the churches. I am the root and the offspring of David, and the bright and morning star. And the Spirit and the bride say, Come. And let him that heareth say, Come. And let him that is athirst come. And whosoever will, let him take the water of life freely' (Revelation 22:12-17).*

You, including all believers, must separate consciously from the corrupt worldly system, preach to others to receive salvation and prepare for eternal life because the time is short.

'But this I say, brethren, the time is short: it remaineth, that both they that have wives be as though they had none; And they that weep, as though they wept not; and they that rejoice, as though they rejoiced not; and they that buy, as though they possessed not; And they that use

this world, as not abusing it: for the fashion of this world passeth away' (1Corinthians 7:29-31).

CHAPTER TEN

PLACE OF WORSHIP

Immediately the church age ended, the door of heaven opened and in a moment, twinkling of an eyes, the saints were caught up. John saw a throne, set in heaven.

'After this I looked, and, behold, a door was opened in heaven: and the first voice which I heard was as it were of a trumpet talking with me; which said, Come up hither, and I will shew thee things which must be hereafter. And immediately I was in the spirit: and, behold, a throne was set in heaven, and one sat on the throne. And he that sat was to look upon like a jasper and a sardine stone: and there was a rainbow round about the throne, in sight like unto an emerald. And round about the throne were four and twenty seats: and upon the seats I saw four and twenty elders sitting, clothed in white raiment; and they had on their heads crowns of gold. And out of the throne proceeded lightnings and thunderings and voices: and there were seven lamps of fire burning before the throne,

which are the seven Spirits of God. And before the throne there was a sea of glass like unto crystal: and in the midst of the throne, and round about the throne, were four beasts full of eyes before and behind' (Revelation 4:1-6).

The heaven referred to is not the atmosphere which surround the globe.

'But the land, whither ye go to possess it, is a land of hills and valleys, and drinketh water of the rain of heaven: And then the LORD'S wrath be kindled against you, and he shut up the heaven, that there be no rain, and that the land yield not her fruit; and lest ye perish quickly from off the good land which the LORD giveth you' (Deuteronomy 11:11).

'For as the heavens are higher than the earth, so are my ways higher than your ways, and my thoughts than your thoughts. For as the rain cometh down, and the snow from heaven, and returneth not thither, but watereth the earth, and maketh it bring forth and bud, that it may give seed to the sower, and bread to the eater: So shall my word be that goeth forth out of my mouth: it shall not return

*unto me void, but it shall accomplish that which I please, and it shall prosper in the thing whereto I sent it' (*Isaiah 55:9-11*).*

*'Who covereth the heaven with clouds, who prepareth rain for the earth, who maketh grass to grow upon the mountains' (*Psalm 147:8*).*

Neither is it the sphere in which the sun and moon and stars appear.

*'And God said, Let there be lights in the firmament of the heaven to divide the day from the night; and let them be for signs, and for seasons, and for days, and years' (*Genesis 1:14*).*

*'And he brought him forth abroad, and said, Look now toward heaven, and tell the stars, if thou be able to number them: and he said unto him, So shall thy seed be' (*Genesis 15:5*).*

*'And, Thou, Lord, in the beginning hast laid the foundation of the earth; and the heavens are the works of thine hands' (*Hebrews 1:10*).*

This heaven is the place where God and the holy angels were set in heaven and one sat on the throne. There was a rainbow round about the throne. And round were 24 seats (thrones). And out of the throne proceeded lightning... And before the throne, there was a sea of glass. And in the midst of the throne and round about the throne were.

'After this I looked, and, behold, a door was opened in heaven: and the first voice which I heard was as it were of a trumpet talking with me; which said, Come up hither, and I will shew thee things which must be hereafter. And immediately I was in the spirit: and, behold, a throne was set in heaven, and one sat on the throne. And he that sat was to look upon like a jasper and a sardine stone: and there was a rainbow round about the throne, in sight like unto an emerald. And round about the throne were four and twenty seats: and upon the seats I saw four and twenty elders sitting, clothed in white raiment; and they had on their heads crowns of gold. And out of the throne proceeded lightnings and thunderings and voices: and there were seven lamps of fire burning before the throne, which are the seven Spirits of God. And before the throne there was a sea of glass like unto crystal: and in the midst *of the throne, and round about the throne, were four beasts full of eyes before and behind' (Revelation 4:1-6).*

The throne is mentioned more than ten times in this chapter. This throne attracted John's attention. All other things centered on the throne. This is God's throne.

'Thy throne, O God, is for ever and ever: the sceptre of thy kingdom is a right sceptre' (Psalms 45:6).

'But the LORD shall endure forever: he hath prepared his throne for judgment. And he shall judge the world in righteousness, he shall minister judgment to the people in uprightness' (Psalms 9:7-8).

'The LORD hath prepared his throne in the heavens; and his kingdom ruleth over all' (Psalm 103:19).

'Thus saith the LORD, The heaven is my throne, and the earth is my footstool: where is the house that ye build unto me? And where is the place of my rest?' (Isaiah 66:1).

'But I say unto you, Swear not at all; neither by heaven; for it is God's throne' (Mathew 5:34).

'And immediately I was in the spirit: and, behold, a throne was set in heaven, and one sat on the throne' (Revelation 4:2).

'And I saw a great white throne, and him that sat on it, from whose face the earth and the heaven fled away; and there was found no place for them' (Revelation 20:11).

'And immediately I was in the spirit: and, behold, a throne was set in heaven, and one sat on the throne. And he that sat was to look upon like a jasper and a sardine stone: and there was a rainbow round about the throne, in sight like unto an emerald' (Revelation 4:2-3).

'And out of the throne proceeded lightnings and thunderings and voices: and there were seven lamps of fire burning before the throne, which are the seven Spirits of God' (Revelation 4:5).

'And the four beasts had each of them six wings about him; and they were full of eyes within: and they rest not day and night, saying, Holy, holy, holy, Lord God Almighty, which was, and is, and is to come' (Revelation 4: 8).

'Thou art worthy, O Lord, to receive glory and honor and power: for thou hast created all things, and for thy pleasure they are and were created' (Revelation 4: 11).

Who is this person that sat on the throne that attracted the whole attention of John and dominated his whole being? Who is this personality that he said looked like a Jasper and a Sardine stone and rainbow about the throne, in sight like unto an emerald? Who is this person that had the power to sit on a throne that produced lightning and thundering, voices with seven lamps of fire burning before the throne, which are seven spirits of God?

A throne like sea of glass and crystal, with four beasts, round about it, filled with eyes, before and behind. Who can approach this throne? Who can battle against this throne and relate with the personality sitting upon the throne? In answer to these questions, He is God, who quickeneth all things, who is blessed and only potentate... who only has immortality... to whom be honor and power everlasting.

John saw the splendor of God's throne and the glory of God. The rainbow round about the throne of God shows God's faithfulness and mercy to the redeemed. This throne is not a throne that comes and goes. It is God's throne with the scepter of His kingdom, a right scepter that lasts forever and ever without stop. This throne of all thrones with all power of all powers without end is greatly great to behold.

> 'Thy throne, O God, is for ever and ever: the sceptre of thy kingdom is a right sceptre' (Psalms 45:6).
>
> 'But the LORD shall endure forever: he hath prepared his throne for judgment. And he shall judge the world in righteousness, he shall minister judgment to the people in uprightness' (Psalms 9:7-8).

God who sat on the throne lasts forever, the throne itself last forever and the throne is prepared for true judgment, righteous judgment that endures forever. If you are experiencing injustice here on earth, approach this throne and He that sat on it. He is the final judge who can judge your judge on earth, reverse every evil judgment, pronouncements against you and give you true justice, righteous justice because He ministers justice to people that come to Him in uprightness.

He is the judge of the world. Other ministries of justice and their ministers are subject to Him. He can reverse the judgment in the Supreme Courts of the nations of the world and get his children free. Lawmakers of all the cities, states and nations of the world are under

Him. This throne can reverse whatever verdict, pronouncement against you.

> *'When a man's ways please the LORD, he maketh even his enemies to be at peace with him' (Proverbs 16:7).*

If you meet His standard, reconcile with Him by repenting and confess your sins, you will obtain justice. Every satanic verdict bows at His pronouncements. This throne is not just in heaven, it is prepared in the heaven of heavens and this kingdom ruleth over all kingdoms. If your attackers, oppressors or your problems are coming from household enemies, witchcraft kingdom, the water kingdom, once you please God, the one that sits on this throne that ruleth over all, you will be delivered.

> *'The LORD hath prepared his throne in the heavens; and his kingdom ruleth over all' (Psalms 103:19).*
>
> *'Thus saith the LORD, The heaven is my throne, and the earth is my footstool: where is the house that ye build unto me? And where is the place of my rest?' (Isaiah 66:1).*

God's throne is in the heaven and the earth and her activities is God's footstool. Make peace with Him, please God and your enemies will bow.

> 'And I saw a great white throne, and him that sat on it, from whose face the earth and the heaven fled away; and there was found no place for them' (Revelation 20:11).

If you have access to this throne, your enemies will not be able to stand against you. It is a throne of peace for those who have relationship with the Prince of Peace. It is a throne of God, who rules and reigns over all. If at the face of He who sits on this throne the earth and heaven ran away, your enemies, problems and all that oppose you will abandon you. If you bring your case file, matters of life to this throne, your enemy's activities over your life will flee away and they will not find any place in your life and whatever you do on earth. The worshippers in this throne are true worshippers, holy worshippers and everlasting worshippers.

> 'And before the throne there was a sea of glass like unto crystal: and in the midst of the throne, and round about the throne, were four beasts full of eyes before and behind.

And the first beast was like a lion, and the second beast like a calf, and the third beast had a face as a man, and the fourth beast was like a flying eagle. And the four beasts had each of them six wings about him; and they were full of eyes within: and they rest not day and night, saying, Holy, holy, holy, Lord God Almighty, which was, and is, and is to come. And when those beasts give glory and honor and thanks to him that sat on the throne, who liveth for ever and ever, The four and twenty elders fall down before him that sat on the throne, and worship him that liveth for ever and ever, and cast their crowns before the throne, saying, Thou art worthy, O Lord, to receive glory and honor and power: for thou hast created all things, and for thy pleasure they are and were created' (*Revelation 4:6-11*).

The first beasts...rest not day and night, saying, holy, holy, Lord God Almighty. Who are these Beasts? Here the word translated Beast in Revelation 13:1.

'And I stood upon the sand of the sea, and saw a beast rise up out of the sea, having seven heads and ten horns, and

upon his horns ten crowns, and upon his heads the name
of blasphemy' (Revelation 13:1).

'The lion' means "vicious, wild Beast" referring to the antichrist. The
four living creatures are representatives of angelic beings.

'Also out of the midst thereof came the likeness of four
living creatures. And this was their appearance; they had
the likeness of a man' (Ezekiel 1:5).

'As for the likeness of their faces, they four had the face of
a man, and the face of a lion, on the right side: and they
four had the face of an ox on the left side; they four also
had the face of an eagle' (Ezekiel 1:10).

'As for the likeness of the living creatures, their
appearance was like burning coals of fire, and like the
appearance of lamps: it went up and down among the
living creatures; and the fire was bright, and out of the fire
went forth lightning. And the living creatures ran and
returned as the appearance of a flash of lightning' (Ezekiel
1:13-14).

In the time of Ezekiel, he saw this four living creatures appeared to him in the likeness of man with lion faces, eagles, burning coals of fire, lamps and flash lighting. All their body, backs, hands, wings, wheels were full of eyes roundabout with four faces. The first face had the face of cherub, the second face was the face of a man, the third face was the face of a lion and the fourth as the face of eagle.

'And their whole body, and their backs, and their hands, and their wings, and the wheels, were full of eyes round about, even the wheels that they four had' (Ezekiel 10:12).

'And every one had four faces: the first face was the face of a cherub, and the second face was the face of a man, and the third the face of a lion, and the fourth the face of an eagle. And the cherubims were lifted up. This is the living creature that I saw by the river of Chebar' (Ezekiel 10:14-15).

'This is the living creature that I saw under the God of Israel by the river of Chebar; and I knew that they were the cherubims' (Ezekiel 10:20).

'In the year that king Uzziah died I saw also the Lord sitting upon a throne, high and lifted up, and his train filled the temple. Above it stood the seraphims: each one

had six wings; with twain he covered his face, and with
twain he covered his feet, and with twain he did fly. And
one cried unto another, and said, Holy, holy, holy, is the
LORD of hosts: the whole earth is full of his glory. And the
posts of the door moved at the voice of him that cried, and
the house was filled with smoke' (Isaiah 6:1-4).

Isaiah also saw this living creatures and everyone that saw it had tremendous change. These are ministering angels before the throne whose ministries are perfect, complete and undefiled. Isaiah saw this throne, the Lord sitting upon it, high and lifted up and His train filled the temple. There are different orders of angels and they all worshipped God, minister to the holiness of God. These four living creatures will be active in executing the judgment of God during the great tribulation

'And I saw when the Lamb opened one of the seals, and I
heard, as it were the noise of thunder, one of the four
beasts saying, Come and see. And I saw, and behold a
white horse: and he that sat on him had a bow; and a
crown was given unto him: and he went forth conquering,
and to conquer. And when he had opened the second seal,

I heard the second beast say, Come and see. And there went out another horse that was red: and power was given to him that sat thereon to take peace from the earth, and that they should kill one another: and there was given unto him a great sword. And when he had opened the third seal, I heard the third beast say, Come and see. And I beheld, and lo a black horse; and he that sat on him had a pair of balances in his hand. And I heard a voice in the midst of the four beasts say, A measure of wheat for a penny, and three measures of barley for a penny; and see thou hurt not the oil and the wine. And when he had opened the fourth seal, I heard the voice of the fourth beast say, Come and see. And I looked, and behold a pale horse: and his name that sat on him was Death, and Hell followed with him. And power was given unto them over the fourth part of the earth, to kill with sword, and with hunger, and with death, and with the beasts of the earth' (Revelation 6:1-8).

And round about the throne were 24 seats, thrones and upon the seats, thrones, I saw 24 elders sitting, clothed in white raiment and they had on their heads crowns of gold. The 24 elders siting, clothed in white raiment; and they had on their heads crown of gold. The 24 elders fall down before Him that sat on the throne and worship

> '*And round about the throne were four and twenty seats: and upon the seats I saw four and twenty elders sitting, clothed in white raiment; and they had on their heads crowns of gold*' (*Revelation 4:4*).

> '*The four and twenty elders fall down before him that sat on the throne, and worship him that liveth for ever and ever, and cast their crowns before the throne, saying...*' (*Revelation 4:10*).

Who are these 24 elders, sitting on the throne In Revelation 4:4?

> '*To him that overcometh will I grant to sit with me in my throne, even as I also overcame, and am set down with my Father in his throne*' (*Revelation 3:21*).

> '*And hast made us unto our God kings and priests: and we shall reign on the earth. And I beheld, and I heard the voice of many angels round about the throne and the beasts and the elders: and the number of them was ten*

thousand times ten thousand, and thousands of thousands' (Revelation 5:10-11).

They were clothed in white raiment and they had on their heads crowns of gold. They are among the saints that overcame, they are the overcomers, they are among the raptured saints, prepared for the marriage of the lamb, ready to be administered for marriage with the lamb, qualified, arrayed in white fine linen, clean, for the linen is the righteousness of saints. They are saints who endured to the end, who escaped from the devil's persecutions, trials and imprisonment, found faithful and now crowned.

They are saints who held their profession fast to the end, representative of all the raptured saints. They are selected among the saints, the raptured saints to sit round the throne of the Almighty, the throne of all thrones with special crowns to worship forever and ever. They are redeemed men; they represent all the redeemed, raptured church. They had harps, golden vials, and full of odors, which are the prayers of saints. They sung a new song.

They are among the raptured saints, made kings, priests and shall reign on earth. They are believers who kept their faith, lively stones, built up a spiritual house, and holy priesthood, to offer sacrifices, acceptable to God by Jesus. They are raptured saints, chosen generation, royal priests, holy, and peculiar, called out of the darkness of the world into the marvelous light that praised God on earth to the end not minding their circumstances.

They were among the rejected people, hated people by the people of the world, people whose rights were trampled upon, people treated in the world without mercy but now they obtained mercy from He that sat on in Revelation 4:4.

'Let us be glad and rejoice, and give honor to him: for the marriage of the Lamb is come, and his wife hath made herself ready. And to her was granted that she should be arrayed in fine linen, clean and white: for the fine linen is the righteousness of saints' (Revelation 19:7-8).

'Fear none of those things which thou shalt suffer: behold, the devil shall cast some of you into prison, that ye may be tried; and ye shall have tribulation ten days: be thou faithful unto death, and I will give thee a crown of life' (Revelation 2:10).

'Behold, I come quickly: hold that fast which thou hast, that no man take thy crown' (Revelation 3:11).

'And when he had taken the book, the four beasts and four and twenty elders fell down before the Lamb, having every one of them harps, and golden vials full of odors,

which are the prayers of saints. [9] And they sung a new song, saying, Thou art worthy to take the book, and to open the seals thereof: for thou wast slain, and hast redeemed us to God by thy blood out of every kindred, and tongue, and people, and nation; [10] And hast made us unto our God kings and priests: and we shall reign on the earth' (Revelation 5:8-10).

'Ye also, as lively stones, are built up a spiritual house, an holy priesthood, to offer up spiritual sacrifices, acceptable to God by Jesus Christ' (1Peter 2:5).

'And a stone of stumbling, and a rock of offence, even to them, which stumble at the word, being disobedient: whereunto also they were appointed. But ye are a chosen generation, a royal priesthood, an holy nation, a peculiar people; that ye should shew forth the praises of him who hath called you out of darkness into his marvelous light: Which in time past were not a people, but are now the people of God: which had not obtained mercy, but now have obtained mercy' (1Peter 2:8-10).

Why are they only 24 elders? Seeing the church as a priesthood, the representatives are the same in number as the priesthood in the time of David, divided into 24 courses

'And David distributed them, both Zadok of the sons of Eleazar, and Ahimelech of the sons of Ithamar, according to their offices in their service' (1Chronicles 24:3-19).

CHAPTER ELEVEN

PRAISE AND WORSHIP LEADERS

These beasts were selected by the government of heaven to lead in praise worship. Each of them had six wings, filled with eyes within. They had no rest, day and night, saying, holy, holy, Lord God Almighty, which was and is and is to come without ceasing. They gave glory, honor and thanks to Him that sat on the throne, who live forever and ever and cast their crowns before the throne saying, thou art worthy, O Lord, to receive glory and honor and power...

In fact, their praise worship was continuous, with joy and unending power, filled with excitement, they worshipped. They do not need rest because the needs for rest disappeared. To stand, sit, and walk or to be in God's presence, before His throne, you need nothing except praise, thanksgiving and honor to Him. People who will have this privilege will not be stopped again by any power.

They had all the mobility they need without being stopped and their speed is faster than the fastest on earth today. They have divine wings, filled with eyes to see everything they need to see. They have power to sing, praise and worship the Almighty without having the need to rest. Their songs are new, undefiled, unknown before and not available to best composers of songs on earth, past, present or future on this earth.

It is a new brand song and only the redeemed that remain righteous on the day of rapture will be involved. Every raptured believer from every kindred, tongue, people and nation will be directly involved. They will respond in unionism to the leaders of the song without tribal, racial or class discrimination. No matter where you came from, your limitations or class on earth, once you made it through rapture, you are a king, priest before God and you will be involved to reign with Christ on earth.

The angels, many of them will be involved to respond to the redeemer's worships to the Almighty. They will stand round about the throne and their number will be up to ten thousand and thousands. That day, Jesus will be honored like never before and Satan, every creature will return to Christ all the power, riches, wisdom, strength, honor, glory and blessings.

Everything good with the devil, his agents and with every creature will be released and returned to Christ in full. Whatever the occult, evil men, wicked people are enjoying now, their riches, glory, greatness will be taken away and returned to Christ. If you will make it to the rapture day, you will be involved in this praise worship. No matter what you are going through today or will ever go through in life will be forgotten in a moment of time before this throne.

All the suffering on earth, the hardship, everything negative heaped on you is worth going through provided you make it to the throne. The memory of failures, defeats and sufferings will vanish the moment you stand before that throne. Jesus will avenge you of everything the devil has ever done against you. We as the redeemed will shout Alleluia before the throne. Joy will enter your bones, marrow as the voice of great multitude like many waters, mighty thundering from among the saints will sing saying Alleluia, for the Lord God Omnipotent reigneth

'And the four beasts had each of them six wings about him; and they were full of eyes within: and they rest not day and night, saying, Holy, holy, holy, Lord God Almighty, which was, and is, and is to come. ⁹ And when those beasts give glory and honor and thanks to him that sat on the throne, who liveth for ever and ever, The four and twenty elders fall down before him that sat on the throne, and worship him that liveth for ever and ever, and cast their crowns before the throne, saying, Thou art worthy, O Lord, to receive glory and honor and power: for thou hast created all things, and for thy pleasure they are and were created' (Revelation 4:8-11).

'And the four beasts said, Amen. And the four and twenty elders fell down and worshipped him that liveth for ever and ever' (Revelation 5:9-14).

'After this I beheld, and, lo, a great multitude, which no man could number, of all nations, and kindreds, and people, and tongues, stood before the throne, and before the Lamb, clothed with white robes, and palms in their hands; And cried with a loud voice, saying, Salvation to our God which sitteth upon the throne, and unto the Lamb. And all the angels stood round about the throne, and about the elders and the four beasts, and fell before the throne on their faces, and worshipped God, Saying, Amen: Blessing, and glory, and wisdom, and thanksgiving, and honor, and power, and might, be unto our God for ever and ever. Amen' (Revelation 7:9-12).

'These have power to shut heaven, that it rain not in the days of their prophecy: and have power over waters to turn them to blood, and to smite the earth with all plagues, as often as they will. Saying, We give thee thanks, O Lord God Almighty, which art, and wast, and art to come; because thou hast taken to thee thy great power, and hast reigned' (Revelation 11:16-17).

'And after these things I heard a great voice of much people in heaven, saying, Alleluia; Salvation, and glory, and honor, and power, unto the Lord our God: For true and righteous are his judgments: for he hath judged the great whore, which did corrupt the earth with her fornication, and hath avenged the blood of his servants at her hand. And again they said, Alleluia. And her smoke rose up for ever and ever. And the four and twenty elders and the four beasts fell down and worshipped God that sat on the throne, saying, Amen; Alleluia. And a voice came out of the throne, saying, Praise our God, all ye his servants, and ye that fear him, both small and great. And I heard as it were the voice of a great multitude, and as the voice of many waters, and as the voice of mighty thunderings, saying, Alleluia: for the Lord God omnipotent reigneth. Let us be glad and rejoice, and give honor to him: for the marriage of the Lamb is come, and his wife hath made herself ready. And to her was granted that she should be arrayed in fine linen, clean and white: for the fine linen is the righteousness of saints. And he saith unto me, Write, Blessed are they which are called unto the marriage supper of the Lamb. And he saith unto me, These are the true sayings of God' (Revelation 19:1-9).

At the end of the ends, God takes the glory while fallen angels and fallen men are banished from heaven. All rebels are out of sight, no more witchcraft, oppression and problem. Holy angels and the redeemed men now worship God. They pour unceasing praise unto God in worship and adoration. This is the culmination of God's redemptive plan. His purpose of creation and redemption is ultimately fulfilled –

> 'Thou art worthy, O Lord, to receive glory and honor and power: for thou hast created all things, and for thy pleasure they are and were created' (Revelation 4:11).

No prayer warriors, marriage committee, building committee, board members or church accountant who handles church money are mentioned. The reason is because there will be no need for those things. Only singers, praise worshippers with the angels, trained to do so are there. Will you be there? To be there, you have to repent, confess all your sins, forsake them and get involved in praising God here on earth, no matter what you go through. Learn how to honor God, praise Him and thank Him, no matter what you are going through. David sang the song of deliverance when he was in fear, danger, trouble and affliction. Learn how to sing in the midst of trouble, fears, dangers and afflictions.

'I will bless the LORD at all times: his praise shall continually be in my mouth. My soul shall make her boast in the LORD: the humble shall hear thereof, and be glad. O magnify the LORD with me, and let us exalt his name together. I sought the LORD, and he heard me, and delivered me from all my fears' (Psalms 34:1-4).

'Many are the afflictions of the righteous: but the LORD delivereth him out of them all' (Psalms 34:19).

The gratitude of the psalmist prompted him thankfully to record the goodness of the Lord. He resolved to bless the Lord at all times, because he knew to whom praise is due and what is due and for what and when. By right of creation and redemption, the Lord has a monopoly in His creatures' praise.

At all times, in every situation, under every circumstance, before, in and after trials, in bright days and dark nights of fears, the Lord deserves our praise and worship. While the people of the world by sight, trust in the arm of the flesh, the people of God should trust in the arm of the Lord, the people of God should trust in the name of the Lord our God.

All who believe in God, praising and gives thanks to Him will rise victorious. God is a holy God; the people that worship Him must be holy. If you cannot praise God here, you will not join the heavenly worshippers after the rapture. To be delivered from the great coming suffering, you have to do everything possible to be raptured. You have to get committed to the work of God after being born again.

Christ gave all for us and left all the glory of heaven that we might be ransomed. There should therefore be nothing too great and no price too high for us as we show our loyalty to God. The early disciples followed Christ and went on to become fishers of men. Paul is the pacesetter in working with God in the New Testament.

To work for God and be raptured:

- You are expected to possess true holiness (Ephesians 4:24, 1Peter 1:14-16, Psalm 15:1-3, 119:172, Proverbs 31:26).

- You must allow the truth to remain as it is in Christ (Ephesians 4:20-21, 1Thessalonians 4:9, 2 John 4).

- You must give no place to the devil (Ephesians 4:27, Luke 11:24-26, 1 Peter 5:8-9).

CHAPTER TWELVE

THE JUDGMENT SEAT OF CHRIST

So far, the church age is gone, a mystery, the rapture of the church is over. In chapter 2 and 3, Christ was on earth talking to the church, represented by the seven churches in Asia. In chapter 4, the heaven opened and received the church, the raptured saints. Where are we now? We are still in heaven, before the throne and He that sat on the throne with a sealed book.

'And I saw in the right hand of him that sat on the throne a book written within and on the backside, sealed with seven seals. And I saw a strong angel proclaiming with a loud voice, Who is worthy to open the book, and to loose the seals thereof?' (Revelation 5:1-2).

EVENT AFTER THE RAPTURE

Immediately the rapture takes place, there would be a gathering of the saints, the angels of ten thousands of thousands before the throne of God beyond and above the heaven where the sun, moon and stars appear. The heaven we talk about is the place where God and His entire holy angels live in. There, God will declare two programs for the raptured saints.

After the rapture, raptured believers would be brought into an examination or judgment before the Lord Jesus. This is known and referred to as appearing before the judgment seat of Christ.

'For we must all appear before the judgment seat of Christ; that every one may receive the things done in his body, according to that he hath done, whether it be good or bad' (2 Corinthians 5:10).

'But why dost thou judge thy brother? Or why dost thou set at nought thy brother? For we shall all stand before the judgment seat of Christ' (Romans 14:10).

This judgment does not consider the salvation of the victim's salvation as whether he is free from sin and worthy to stand before

God or not. All the raptured believers are free from sin before the rapture.

> 'There is therefore now no condemnation to them which are in Christ Jesus, who walk not after the flesh, but after the Spirit' (Roman 8:1).

> 'Verily, verily, I say unto you, He that heareth my word, and believeth on him that sent me, hath everlasting life, and shall not come into condemnation; but is passed from death unto life' (John 5:24).

> 'Herein is our love made perfect, that we may have boldness in the Day of Judgment: because as he is, so are we in this world' (1 John 4:17).

When you are born-again and forsake your sins, God has promised he would remember your sins and iniquities no more.

> 'And their sins and iniquities will I remember no more' Hebrews 10:17...

The first stage of judgment or test is for our life on earth because that is what will qualify anyone for the rapture. God's first interest on every one of us is on whom we are, not what we do. It is after you live your life here on earth for God and you are raptured that you would qualify for this judgment. Therefore, you must work with good character, the fruits of the Spirit and eternity in view.

The reason for this judgment or examination is to know your reward, how to reward you (*see* 1 Corinthians 3:6-15). Not all that made it through the rapture will be rewarded equal. Rewards will be given according to how you work by God's wisdom. It is not going to be according to the volume or quantity of work you did but according to the grace given to you. Believers are going to be rewarded on how much they used their talent or opportunity to work on earth. You will be rewarded on how careful, diligent, discipline and how determined, the effort you put to do what God assigned to you. The quality of work done according to God's laid down rules is going to be considered. Every work you did to God will be tested by fire and you will be judged or rewarded based on the quantity of work that survived the test of fire.

'I have planted, Apollos watered; but God gave the increase' (1Corinthians 3:6).

'Now if any man build upon this foundation gold, silver, precious stones, wood, hay, stubble; Every man's work shall be made manifest: for the day shall declare it, because it shall be revealed by fire; and the fire shall try every man's work of what sort it is. If any man's work abide which he hath built thereupon, he shall receive a reward. If any man's work shall be burned, he shall suffer loss: but he himself shall be saved; yet so as by fire' (1 Corinthians 3:12-15).

Some believers work may suffer loss because of carelessness, neglect or not using their talents fully well. It is not a judgment that will lead any raptured believer to hell, no, not at all. Another word for judgment seat of Christ is Bema, which is translated judgment seat, meaning reward seat. This judgment for reward will take place between the rapture and the revelation of Christ to the earth. It will take place in the air, before God's presence, in the sphere of heavens.

'Then we which are alive and remain shall be caught up together with them in the clouds, to meet the Lord in the air: and so shall we ever be with the Lord' (1Thessalonians 4:17).

'It is reported commonly that there is fornication among you, and such fornication as is not so much as named among the Gentiles, that one should have his father's wife. And ye are puffed up, and have not rather mourned, that he that hath done this deed might be taken away from among you. For I verily, as absent in body, but present in spirit, have judged already, as though I were present, concerning him that hath so done this deed, In the name of our Lord Jesus Christ, when ye are gathered together, and my spirit, with the power of our Lord Jesus Christ, To deliver such an one unto Satan for the destruction of the flesh, that the spirit may be saved in the day of the Lord Jesus. Your glorying is not good. Know ye not that a little leaven leaveneth the whole lump? Purge out therefore the old leaven, that ye may be a new lump, as ye are unleavened. For even Christ our Passover is sacrificed for us: Therefore let us keep the feast, not with old leaven, neither with the leaven of malice and wickedness; but with the unleavened bread of sincerity and truth' (1 Corinthians 5:1-8).*

Believer's real inheritance is not in this earth but in the heavens. Believers focus, investment must be on things that have heavens

254 • Prayer M. Madueke

attachment. Everything a believer do must be done with eternity in view. In the judgment bema seat, Jesus Christ will be the judge and will give reward to each believer according to his or her works.

'For we must all appear before the judgment seat of Christ; that every one may receive the things done in his body, according to that he hath done, whether it be good or bad' (2 Corinthians 5:10).

'For the Father judgeth no man, but hath committed all judgment unto the Son' (John 5:22).

'But why dost thou judge thy brother? Or why dost thou set at nought thy brother? For we shall all stand before the judgment seat of Christ' (Romans 14:10).

'He that hath an ear, let him hear what the Spirit saith unto the churches; To him that overcometh will I give to eat of the tree of life, which is in the midst of the paradise of God' (Revelation 2:7).

'He that hath an ear, let him hear what the Spirit saith unto the churches; To him that overcometh will I give to eat of the hidden manna, and will give him a white stone, and in the stone a new name written, which no man knoweth saving he that receiveth it' (Revelation 2:17).

'But that which ye have already hold fast till I come. And he that overcometh, and keepeth my works unto the end, to him will I give power over the nations: And he shall rule them with a rod of iron; as the vessels of a potter shall they be broken to shivers: even as I received of my Father. And I will give him the morning star' (Revelation 2:25-28).

'Behold, I come quickly: hold that fast which thou hast, that no man take thy crown' (Revelation 3:11).

'And I John saw the holy city, new Jerusalem, coming down from God out of heaven, prepared as a bride adorned for her husband' (Revelation 21:2).

'And to the angel of the church in Pergamos write; These things saith he which hath the sharp sword with two edges; I know thy works, and where thou dwellest, even where Satan's seat is: and thou holdest fast my name, and hast not denied my faith, even in those days wherein Antipas was my faithful martyr, who was slain among you, where Satan dwelleth. But I have a few things against thee, because thou hast there them that hold the doctrine of Balaam, who taught Balac to cast a stumbling block before the children of Israel, to eat things sacrificed unto *idols, and to commit fornication. So hast thou also them that hold the doctrine of the Nicolaitans, which thing I hate. Repent; or else I will come unto thee quickly, and will fight against them with the sword of my mouth. He that hath an ear, let him hear what the Spirit saith unto the churches; To him that overcometh will I give to eat of the hidden manna, and will give him a white stone, and in the stone a new name written, which no man knoweth saving he that receiveth it' (Revelation 2:12-16).*

Different rewards Christ would give include the following:

1. The overcomers crown, an incorruptible crown (1 Corinthians 9:25).

2. The soul winners crown, crown of rejoicing (1 Thessalonians 2:19, Daniel 12:3).

3. Crown of life, for tried and triumphant saints (James 1:12).

4. Crown of righteousness, for loving His appearance (2 Timothy 4:8).

5. Crown of glory, for feeding the flock of God (1 Peter 5:4).

These rewards will position each believer, place him in his place in the kingdom and prepare him for the marriage supper of the saints.

CHAPTER THIRTEEN

THE MARRIAGE SUPPER OF THE LAMB

This marriage speaks of the eternal union between Christ and the believers, the raptured church.

'Let us be glad and rejoice, and give honor to him: for the marriage of the Lamb is come, and his wife hath made herself ready. And to her was granted that she should be arrayed in fine linen, clean and white: for the fine linen is the righteousness of saints' (Revelation 19:7-8).

It is an event that has particular reference to the raptured church and that will be God's second program for the raptured church in heaven (John 3:29, Romans 7:4, 2 Corinthians 11:2, Ephesians 5:22-23, Revelation 19:7-8, 21:1-22).

The bridegroom is our Savior and Lord, Jesus Christ Himself referred to Himself as the bridegroom in the gospel of Matthew chapter nine verse fourteen and fifteen (John 3:27-30, 2 Corinthians 11:2, Ephesians 5:25-27, 32).

Believers who by God's grace were raptured are the bride. (Revelation 19:7-8, 2 Corinthians 11:2).

Israel would be restored. So, no restored wife would be called a virgin. The church is the chaste virgin presented to Christ (2 Corinthians 11:2).

Who are the blessed guests? (Revelation 19:9-10, John 3:28-29, Luke 13:28-29).

All other saints, Old Testament saints, believers martyred during the great tribulation, end time redeemed Israel and Gentiles, apart from the church form the invited guest or those called unto the marriage supper of the Lamb.

CHAPTER FOURTEEN

THE SEVEN-SEALED SCROLL

John saw in the right hand of Him that sat on the heavenly throne a book. This was after the rapture because God's program for the church was shifted to heaven. All the raptured believers now appeared in heaven before this throne and He that sat on it.

> 'And I saw in the right hand of him that sat on the throne a book written within and on the backside, sealed with seven seals' (*Revelation 5:1*).

> 'And when I looked, behold, an hand was sent unto me; and, lo, a roll of a book was therein; And he spread it before me; and it was written within and without: and there was written therein lamentations, and mourning, and woe' (*Ezekiel 2:9-10*).

This book, actually a scroll, written within and on the backside, was rolled up and sealed seven times. A seal was a device, often made with wax and having an imprint pushed upon it which forbade an unauthorized person from opening it. Once broken, a seal was impossible to repair perfectly. So, this seven-sealed book has never been opened and the contents were full of lamentations, mourning and woes. The one that John saw was a full booklet with seven sealed chapters written within and without, sealed with seven seals, closed up and the content was unknown. It is very dangerous to have a seal containing information about you, your family, community, city, people or nation without being able to access its content. Many people are living without the full detail of why they are living.

'And the king appointed them a daily provision of the king's meat, and of the wine which he drank: so nourishing them three years, that at the end thereof they might stand before the king. Now among these were of the children of Judah, Daniel, Hananiah, Mishael, and Azariah: Unto whom the prince of the eunuchs gave names: for he gave unto Daniel the name of Belteshazzar; and to Hananiah, of Shadrach; and to Mishael, of Meshach; and to Azariah, of Abed-nego' (Daniel 5:5-7).

When King Belshazzar saw a man's hand with fingers wrote against him upon the plaster of the wall of the king's palace, he was greatly disturbed. His countenance was changed and his thoughts troubled him. His joint, lions were loosed and his knees smote against each other. He cried aloud for help. He needed an interpreter, someone who is capable of reading the writing, show him the interpretation.

Many people on this earth do not know their purpose on earth and they are not bordered or worried. Yet, both God and the devil have written so many things concerning them. To be born again is good but you have to know God's master plan for your life; what He wants you to do on earth. You have to be able to have access to His written will, interpret it and apply them here on earth before you die.

The bible is God's will for every man, but you have to discover personally, what God wants you to achieve from birth to death. You are not born to beat about the bush or to live by the will of the devil. You have to show concern, get worried, and make research through prayer to know why you are here. Belshazzar cried, made effort to discover what was written against him. Though he sought for help in a wrong way, from astrologers, soothsayers and later from the right source.

The important thing was that he never gave up until he discovered the meaning. You may have been struggling in life, looking for the interpretation of certain things in your life, do not give up. Paul spent good number of years trying to find why he was created, God's purpose for creating him.

'For ye have heard of my conversation in time past in the Jews' religion, how that beyond measure I persecuted the church of God, and wasted it: And profited in the Jews' religion above many my equals in mine own nation, being more exceedingly zealous of the traditions of my fathers. But when it pleased God, who separated me from my mother's womb, and called me by his grace, To reveal his Son in me, that I might preach him among the heathen; immediately I conferred not with flesh and blood' (Galatians 1:13-16).

He made so many mistakes but he never gave up. He tried it in the Jews religion, persecuted Christians beyond measure. He profited in the Jews religion above many of his equals. He was so zealous to keep to the traditions of his fathers. He was circumcised on the eight day of the stock of Israel, of the tribe of Benjamin, a Hebrew of Hebrews and a Pharisee. Though, he went the wrong way but God knew he was sincere. If you have not found Christ, you have found nothing and achieved nothing. Your foundation, where you are born is very important. Paul left his foundational bondage the day he found Christ.

'Concerning zeal, persecuting the church; touching the righteousness which is in the law, blameless' (<u>Philippians 3:6</u>).

'But when it pleased God, who separated me from my mother's womb, and called me by his grace, To reveal his Son in me, that I might preach him among the heathen; immediately I conferred not with flesh and blood' (<u>Galatians 1:15-16</u>).

Paul was living in self-righteousness that was of the law, the traditions of the Jews. But when he found Christ, immediately, he conferred not with flesh and blood. If you are still living in sin, depending upon your own way or religion, you are observing the seal of the devil. You need to break out from the evil pattern of your place of birth or church tradition that contradicts God's word.

'Beware lest any man spoil you through philosophy and vain deceit, after the tradition of men, after the rudiments of the world, and not after Christ' (<u>Colossian 2:8</u>).

'And he spake many things unto them in parables, saying, Behold, a sower went forth to sow; And when he sowed,

some seeds fell by the way side, and the fowls came and devoured them up' (Matthew 13:3-4).

If you are born or sown where fornication, violence, murder or any character devours people's life, destiny, you need to search for God's plan. It is not God's will for poverty or any problem to devour your life; you are under Satan's seal. If you are born or you fell on wrong place, hard foundation, where you have just little or no opportunity to survive, you are under Satan's seal. It is not God's will for the sun to scorch your destiny or to cause your root to be withered.

'Some fell upon stony places, where they had not much earth: and forthwith they sprung up, because they had no deepness of earth: And when the sun was up, they were scorched; and because they had no root, they withered away. And some fell among thorns; and the thorns sprung up, and choked them' (Matthew 13:5-7).

There are people that were born in your family, they lived and died under the scorch of sun. At the prime of their lives, they withered away from the root. Some were choked because they fell among thorns. Even those born in good families, Christian foundation by

Christian parents, because they could not put much effort, they fail to score pass mark.

> 'But other fell into good ground, and brought forth fruit, some an hundredfold, some sixtyfold, some thirtyfold' (*Matthew 13:8*).

To agree with the devil, and continue in sin when Christ had died for you, is the worst foolishness.

> 'And I heard, but I understood not: then said I, O my Lord, what shall be the end of these things? And he said, Go thy way, Daniel: for the words are closed up and sealed till the time of the end' (*Daniel 12:8-9*).

Believers, everyone in this earth must ask question, questions that will lead you to know your foundation, beginning and your end. It is not enough to be born again, you need to press forward, fight and resist evil forces. Daniel was a true child of God but he was not satisfied with the situation he found himself. His nation was not progressing; they were out of God's plan, purpose and place of assignment.

He wanted to see the end, know the end and possibly what to do. Christian life is likened to warfare, wrestling and fight to discover your destiny, why you are here on earth and possibly what to do. It is a disgrace for a Christian or anyone to die under Satan's will or seal. From what we see in the judgment seat of Christ, the bema judgment, many believers will lose their reward; their works on earth will be burnt by fire.

The book of Revelation we are studying is future and a warning to both saints and sinners. There is a case file opened with your name by God and Satan. You have to choose the one you want to be implemented in your life and for your life. If you remain a sinner, a prayer less Christian, you have made a choice. If you are born again, forsake your sins, you have equally made a choice, so start fighting to obtain a price even as a Christian. You can close up Satan's case file against you or decide to live by it as a Christian.

'And when he had opened the seventh seal, there was silence in heaven about the space of half an hour' (*Revelation 8:1*).

We have seen God's scroll for raptured believers in our first chapter. It unfolded two major events that will take place for the period of seven years, the judgment seat of Christ and the marriage supper of the lamb. What we are looking at is the seal for those who fail to rapture on earth. What is going to happen to them for the next seven years immediately after rapture? None of these things has happened, so anyone can decide where he wants to be. Scroll in this document, which determined the climax of human history, is yet to be implemented. Inside the scroll, on the backside are the seven stages of the end of man's day on earth. From chapter 6 to chapter 19, the seven stages, one at a time, unfold. When the scroll is unfolded, opened and revealed, what happens? That is the beginning of the great tribulation.

'And I saw when the Lamb opened one of the seals, and I heard, as it were the noise of thunder, one of the four beasts saying, Come and see. And I saw, and behold a white horse: and he that sat on him had a bow; and a crown was given unto him: and he went forth conquering, and to conquer. And when he had opened the second seal, I heard the second beast say, Come and see. And there went out another horse that was red: and power was given to him that sat thereon to take peace from the earth, and *that they should kill one another: and there was given unto him a great sword. And when he had opened the third seal, I heard the third beast say, Come and see. And I beheld, and lo a black horse; and he that sat on him had a pair of balances in his hand. And I heard a voice in the midst of the four beasts say, A measure of wheat for a penny, and three measures of barley for a penny; and see thou hurt not the oil and the wine. And when he had opened the fourth seal, I heard the voice of the fourth beast say, Come and see' (Revelation 6:1-7).*

In the time of Daniel, what shall be the end of these things was closed up and sealed until the time of the end. The sealed scroll is in the hand of God. Finally, man's day ends, Christ returns in power to establish God's day on earth in the form of the millennial kingdom.

CHAPTER FIFTEEN

THE LAMB OF GOD

The book of Revelation Chapter 5 is a continuation of chapter 4 and it is a critical chapter, a crucial point in the book of Revelation. This chapter is very important, as it is the key to the rest of the book of Revelation. With the church age gone, the mystery which is the rapture of the church gone, the heaven opened and a throne in sight, we are about to enter a new phase. In the first seven years after the rapture, God has no program for the raptured saints here on earth. Their portion is in heaven. The bema judgment and the marriage supper of the lamb is God's program for the saints and it is in heaven. Haven seen the seven seals, the heaven is looking for who is worthy to open it, read and interpret what is therein.

'And I saw a strong angel proclaiming with a loud voice, Who is worthy to open the book, and to loose the seals thereof? And no man in heaven, nor in earth, neither under the earth, was able to open the book, neither to look thereon. And I wept much, because no man was found

worthy to open and to read the book, neither to look thereon' (Revelation 5:2-4).

The assignment to proclaim, search for the worthy one to receive the book, open the book and loose the seals thereof was not given to an ordinary angel, but a strong angel. He was assigned, empowered to execute the assignment with a loud voice so that every creature in heaven and earth, under the earth will hear. He obeyed and did as he was commanded, unfortunately; no man in heaven or in earth, neither under the earth was able to open the book, neither to look thereon. It was a big disappointment, a woeful failure that God has a program, sealed up, but none among the creature was found worthy to approach God's throne, His presence to receive God's program for mankind.

The multitudes sinners living on earth and the entire raptured saints have no access for the end. It was a big vacuum, a failure among human. The same thing is applicable today in many organizations, communities, families and nations. Every problem on earth today has a solution attached to them, sealed and waiting for a qualified person to be able to approach God, receive it, and lose it to help humanity.

There are things, situation and level that no one has reached in your family, community and all places but none is unreachable. If you can pray, get closer to God and ask for power to receive, loose, you will take your family, group or nation to the next level. What is going on in every family, places and nations in the world calls for weeping before God.

John on seeing the document that contains God's program for human kind but none was qualified, able, fit and proper to receive, loose the seals started weeping. He was allowed to weep, he cried out and with all his strength, his cry was not able to solve the problem. God allowed him to cry until he cried enough, wept much to prove to him that cries cannot solve the problem.

Many people, including believers in many families, are presently weeping because of the situation they found themselves. Many people, families and nations had wept before. They lived and died without achieving anything or dislodging their Goliaths.

John succeeding because before he started weeping, he got to the throne of God. He did not weep before Domitian, the Emperor; he wept before the throne of all thrones, the God of all gods, the Alpha and Omega, the Almighty God.

'All we like sheep have gone astray; we have turned everyone to his own way; and the LORD hath laid on him the iniquity of us all' (Isaiah 53:6).

'For all have sinned, and come short of the glory of God'

(Romans 3:23).

He wept before the King of kings, the arm of the Lord. John was an aged believer but he bulldozed himself before the throne of God in the third heaven, before the root of all tender plant, the root that broke forth out of a dry ground, the despised and rejected king of the whole earth. He wept before the one that was acquainted with grief, that carried our sorrows away, bore our grief and was wounded for our transgression.

John wept before the one that was bruised for our iniquity, chastised of our peace, given hot stripes for our sickness, the one that everyone turned away from, who carried the iniquity of mankind. He wept before the one that was oppressed, afflicted for our sake, yet He opened not His mouth. His old age, position as a church leader, insults, persecution from the head of the government, Emperor Domitian, the boiling oil and the unfriendly cold weather from the Isle of Patmos could not stop him from reaching to the throne. Don't allow anything stop you from approaching Christ for your salvation and the liberation of your people, press forward.

When he got there, he wept for solution, for deliverance and for God's last information for the unraptured multitudes of the earth. He wept because man's sin on earth blocked them and denied them access to the throne, access to information that leads to deliverance. He wept because the day of God's anger to trample upon the multitudes of sinners in the world was despised. Salvation has come and none is informed.

He wept because God's fury, vengeance was released but the devil kept them away and engaged people in eating and drinking in sin. As he was weeping before the throne of all thrones, something happened. Where are you weeping now, and where do you always weep when there is problem? When the nation's economy, health sector and security department have problem, where do you normally go to weep? Whom do you normally consult when there is problem? Are you born again, an idol worshipper, occult member, and churchgoer without relationship with Christ?

John overcame all persecution, ignored all pains and wept before the throne. He wept before the greatest titleholder, before He that has the sharp sword with two edges, the great I am that I am, He that liveth and was dead and behold, all of a sudden, He became alive for evermore. The one that has the keys of hell and death, that holds the seven stars in His right hand, the first and the last, the holy one, the truth, the faithful and true witness. What was the result of his weeping, his cries and approach to He that sat on the throne?

'And one of the elders saith unto me, Weep not: behold, the Lion of the tribe of Juda, the Root of David, hath prevailed to open the book, and to loose the seven seals thereof. And I beheld, and, lo, in the midst of the throne and of the four beasts, and in the midst of the elders, stood a Lamb as it had been slain, having seven horns and seven eyes, which are the seven Spirits of God sent forth into all the earth. And he came and took the book out of the right hand of him that sat upon the throne' (Revelation 5:5-7).

John wept because the terrible plagues containing God's program for sinners on earth was in a scroll, book that was covered. God gave the revelation to show and reveal His plans, purpose and the coming event but now, the sealed book containing unfolded, unrevealed mysteries of last events, could not be opened. But something happened; the Lion of all lions, the Lion of the tribe of Judah emerged, appeared, manifested, and showed up. The root of David surfaced again.

'And one of the elders saith unto me, Weep not: behold, the Lion of the tribe of Juda, the Root of David, hath

prevailed to open the book, and to loose the seven seals thereof' (Revelation 5:5).

'*As we have therefore opportunity, let us do good unto all men, especially unto them who are of the household of faith' (Genesis 49:10).*

'*I Jesus have sent mine angel to testify unto you these things in the churches. I am the root and the offspring of David, and the bright and morning star' (Revelation 22:16).*

'*And there shall come forth a rod out of the stem of Jesse, and a Branch shall grow out of his roots: And the spirit of the LORD shall rest upon him, the spirit of wisdom and understanding, the spirit of counsel and might, the spirit of knowledge and of the fear of the LORD; And shall make him of quick understanding in the fear of the LORD: and he shall not judge after the sight of his eyes, neither reprove after the hearing of his ears: But with righteousness shall he judge the poor, and reprove with equity for the meek of the earth: and he shall smite the earth with the rod of his mouth, and with the breath of his lips shall he slay the wicked' (Isaiah 11:1-4).*

'The next day John seeth Jesus coming unto him, and saith, Behold the Lamb of God, which taketh away the sin of the world' (John 1:29).

'And looking upon Jesus as he walked, he saith, Behold the Lamb of God!' (John 1:36).

The lamb slain, yet standing, who is the worthy one, Jesus Christ. What qualified Him? For thou wast slain and hast redeemed us to God (*see* Revelation 5:9, Daniel 7:13-14).

He is the only one that was qualified because He has complete authority, seven horns and seven eyes, which are the seven Spirits of God, sent forth into all the earth. He came, took the book out of the right hand of Him that sat upon the throne. This brought a new song by the four and twenty elders and the four beasts. They fell down before the Lamb with harps, golden vials, full of odors, which are the prayers of the saints. In their songs, they told Jesus, thou art worthy to take the book, to open the seals and tell the world who fail to rapture what they will suffer.

Jesus was and still is the only one who is qualified to approach God, the Ancient of days and received dominion, glory and kingdom to rule and reign over all people, nations and languages of the world forever and ever. God the father is in support of His authority and have given Him power for the whole world to serve Him because His dominion is everlasting. His kingdom will never be stopped or destroyed; it is forever and ever.

'John bare witness of him, and cried, saying, This was he of whom I spake, He that cometh after me is preferred before me: for he was before me' ([John 1:15](#)).

'Wherefore God also hath highly exalted him, and given him a name which is above every name' ([Philippians 2:9](#)).

John the Baptist in His witness concerning Him said, He that cometh after me is preferred before me, for He was before me. Christ was born before every human being, everything because He is the first born of every creation. He is qualified to take the book from God's hand, open the seals thereof because God has exalted Him, gave Him a name, which is far above every other name.

'Being made so much better than the angels, as he hath by inheritance obtained a more excellent name than they. For unto which of the angels said he at any time, Thou art my Son, this day have I begotten thee? And again, I will be

to him a Father, and he shall be to me a Son? And again, when he bringeth in the first begotten into the world, he saith, And let all the angels of God worship him' (Hebrews 1:4-6).

'But to which of the angels said he at any time, Sit on my right hand, until I make thine enemies thy footstool? Are they not all ministering spirits, sent forth to minister for them who shall be heirs of salvation?' (Hebrews 1:13-14).

He is worthy, selected to receive the book, open the seals, read and interpret the things thereof because He is the only one, far much better than the angels put together and by inheritance, He has a more excellent name than all the angels. All angels worship Him, serve Him, respect and honor Him as the first begotten into the world.

'And when he had taken the book, the four beasts and four and twenty elders fell down before the Lamb, having every one of them harps, and golden vials full of odors, which are the prayers of saints. And they sung a new song, saying, Thou art worthy to take the book, and to open the seals thereof: for thou wast slain, and hast redeemed us to

God by thy blood out of every kindred, and tongue, and people, and nation; And hast made us unto our God kings and priests: and we shall reign on the earth. And I beheld, and I heard the voice of many angels round about the throne and the beasts and the elders: and the number of them was ten thousand times ten thousand, and thousands of thousands; Saying with a loud voice, Worthy is the Lamb that was slain to receive power, and riches, and wisdom, and strength, and honor, and glory, and blessing. And every creature which is in heaven, and on the earth, and under the earth, and such as are in the sea, and all that are in them, heard I saying, Blessing, and honor, and glory, and power, be unto him that sitteth upon the throne, and unto the Lamb for ever and ever. And the four beasts said, Amen. And the four and twenty elders fell down and worshipped him that liveth for ever and ever' (Revelation 5:8-14).

Not only the four beasts, the twenty-four elders, but it includes the whole redeemed, they all fell down and sing a new song in worship of the lamb. Everyone without exception with harps shall offer seven fold praise and worship to our redeemer, the Great God on the throne. Men, angels and all creatures shall praise Him.

'Rejoice in the LORD, O ye righteous: for praise is comely for the upright. Praise the LORD with harp: sing unto him with the psaltery and an instrument of ten strings. Sing unto him a new song; play skilfully with a loud noise' (Psalm 33:1-3).

He made us kings, priests and rulers to reign on the earth. The number of His worshippers was ten thousand times ten thousand and thousands of thousands. All they were saying is; worthy is the Lamb that was slain to receive power, riches, wisdom, strength, honor, glory and blessing. With such thundering voices of these singers, every creature in heaven, earth, under the earth, the sea and everything in them heard their voice. They were saying, so at the end of ends, our redeemer and Savior has finally receive all the blessings, honor, glory, and power forever and ever. When the four beasts heard it, they said, Amen, they fell down and worshipped Him that liveth forever and ever.

Finally, finally, the devil bowed and released all the blessings, honor, and glory, power to Him that sitteth upon the throne and unto the Lamb forever and ever. The worst thing that can happen to anyone is to remain in sin, refuse to repent, pursue anything on earth, serve the devil and ignore the gift of salvation. Whatever blessing, honor, glory, or power you can get without Christ is frustration and destructive. Riches, power to achieve anything good, the strength, wisdom and all good things on earth you are pursuing without God is useless and unprofitably disappointing. At the end, every disunity, lies, disagreement and misunderstanding will be put away among the redeemed. Before the throne, after the rapture, the saints will enjoy perfect unity together.

The devil may defile it now, pollute the love of the brethren but it will die before the throne.

> 'After this I beheld, and, lo, a great multitude, which no man could number, of all nations, and kindreds, and people, and tongues, stood before the throne, and before the Lamb, clothed with white robes, and palms in their hands; And cried with a loud voice, saying, Salvation to our God which sitteth upon the throne, and unto the Lamb. And all the angels stood round about the throne, and about the elders and the four beasts, and fell before the throne on their faces, and worshipped God, Saying, Amen: Blessing, and glory, and wisdom, and thanksgiving, and honor, and power, and might, be unto our God forever and ever. Amen' (Revelation 7:9-12).

The redeemed saints, a great multitude of all the nations, kindred, people and tongues will not be stopped. They will stand one day before God's throne, free from oppression and oppressors. They will stand before the throne, freed from witches and wizards, household wickedness and all evil forces before the lamb, clothed with white robes and palms in their hands. They will in perfect unity, full of love and joy sing saying, salvation to our God, which sitteth upon the throne and unto the lamb. As they sing, praise with tears of joy, all the angels will stand round about the throne, the elders; the four beasts will fall before the throne on their faces and worship God.

As they do so, they will be saying amen, blessing, glory, wisdom, thanksgiving, honor, power and might be unto our God forever and ever without any left for the devil and his agents. Amen

'And there were in the same country shepherds abiding in the field, keeping watch over their flock by night. And, lo, the angel of the Lord came upon them, and the glory of the Lord shone round about them: and they were sore afraid. And the angel said unto them, Fear not: for, behold, I bring you good tidings of great joy, which shall be to all people. For unto you is born this day in the city of David a Savior, which is Christ the Lord. And this shall be a sign

unto you; Ye shall find the babe wrapped in swaddling clothes, lying in a manger. And suddenly there was with the angel a multitude of the heavenly host praising God, and saying, Glory to God in the highest, and on earth peace, good will toward men' (Luke 2:8-14).

These angels had sung before when Jesus was born in Judah, unto the city of David, which is called Bethlehem. That day, the glory of the Lord shone round about the shepherds abiding in the field, keeping watch over their flock by night. At the appearance of God's angels, they became afraid.

The angels calmed them down and told them not to fear. You may have any reason to be afraid because of many problems around you now. But if you make peace with Christ, all fear will go, vanish and abandon your life. The angels said to the fearful and fearing shepherds, fear not, for behold, I bring you good tidings of great joy, everlasting joy which shall be for all people. If you give your life to Christ now, Christ will be born into your life. You can receive the Prince of peace into your life and if you keep that faith to the end, you will join these singers to sing a new song before the throne of God that day.

In fact, you will spend eternity praising and worshipping our Redeemer and the great God on the throne. If you refuse and remain in sin and the rapture takes place or you die in sin, you will miss it. If you miss it, you will spend eternity in hell, suffering without an end. The book of Revelation chapter 5 ends God's program on earth and opened the gate of Heaven for the saints before the throne. The rest of the book from chapter six will open the seals, God's program for the multitude that could not rapture. The seals will unfold great suffering, great tribulation and deceptions. Watch out for the rest of the chapters.

'If thou hast run with the footmen, and they have wearied thee, then how canst thou contend with horses? And if in the land of peace, wherein thou trustedst, they wearied thee, then how wilt thou do in the swelling of Jordan?' (*Jeremiah 12:5*).

If you cannot serve God now, pray to God now, abandon sin now, reject idolatry now, it will be more difficult then. If you cannot say no to evil now, reject the blessing from the devil, his glory, honor, wisdom, strength, the power and positions he offer, it will be more difficult then. All good things the devil can offer you now, be it riches, power will be lost immediately after the rapture, at death or even before you die. They will be surrendered to Christ and not only that, whatever power or thing he has now is not up to one percent of what Christ has now, yet whatever he has, though corrupt, belong to Christ.

I do not know why people go to God, insist on sin and refuse to repent. You have choice to make today and decide where you want to spend your eternity with devil or Christ? Good a thing, none of these things has expired, the church age is on, the rapture has not taken place, and you are still alive and can take decision now. The opportunity to sing with the angels, the four beasts and the twenty-four elders are staring at you. You can join the saints now, the door is open, and Christ is knocking at your heart's door. The choice is yours.

SELECTED DECREES

Grace to serve my generation according to God's will, possess me, in the name of Jesus. Anointing to finish well on earth and make heaven, possess me. Power to join heavenly worshippers, possess me forever, in the name of Jesus. Heavenly door closed against me, open by divine mercy. Almighty God, take me to your throne after my life on earth, in the name of Jesus. Power to fly above the atmospheric heaven to the third heaven, possess me, in the name of Jesus. Every organized darkness against my heavenly candidacy, be disorganized, in the name of Jesus.

Almighty God that quickeneth all things, quicken my spiritual life, in the name of Jesus. Any spiritual abortion that need to take place for me to make heaven, take place now. Anointing to honor God forever, fall upon me, in the name of Jesus. You my eternal destiny under satanic arrest, be released. Any evil throne against God's throne working against me, be destroyed, in the name of Jesus. Almighty God, by your mercy, deliver me from every suffering. Hell fire, listen to me, I separate myself forever from you, in the name of Jesus.

I command every glory due for God in the hands of the enemy to be released to God now, in the name of Jesus.

Every rebellious spirit working against my destiny, I banish you forever, in the name of Jesus.

Anointing for an unceasing praise to God, possess me, in the name of Jesus. Power to worship and adore God now and forever, take over me. Let the culmination of God's redemptive plan manifest in my life, in the name of Jesus. You my body, soul and spirit, abort every property of hell fire in you.

Let the purpose of creation and redemption be fulfilled in my life positively, in the name of Jesus. O Lord, keep me holy in the moment of the rapture or death. Almighty God, by your mercy, deliver me from all kinds of tribulation, in the name of Jesus.

THANK YOU!

I wanted to take this opportunity to appreciate you for supporting my ministry and writing career by purchasing my book. I'm a full-time author and every copy of my book bought helps tremendously in supporting my family and that I continue to have the energy and motivation to write. My family and I are very grateful and we don't take your support lightly.

You've done so much for me already but I need you to do me one more favor if you can spare a moment of your time. Please I need you to go to the link below and give me your honest review. This is important because it helps me sell more books.

CLICK HERE TO LEAVE A REVIEW

Please note that I read and appreciate every feedback. Also note that you do not have to have finished reading the book before you can leave a review. You can just share with me what you think of what you've read so far. You can always come back later if you wish and update your review.

Once again, here is the link:

CLICK HERE TO LEAVE A REVIEW

Thank you so much as you spare this precious moment of your time and may God bless you and meet you at every point of your need.

Please send me an email on prayermadu@yahoo.com if you encounter any difficulty in leaving your review.

Other Books by Prayer Madueke

1. 100 Days Prayers to Wake Up Your Lazarus

2. 15 Deliverance Steps to Everlasting Life

3. 21/40 Nights of Decrees and Your Enemies Will Surrender

4. 35 Deliverance Steps to Everlasting Rest

5. 35 Special Dangerous Decrees

6. 40 Prayer Giants

7. Alone with God

8. Americans, May I Have Your Attention Please

9. Avoid Academic Defeats

10. Because You Are Living Abroad

11. Biafra of My Dream

12. Breaking Evil Yokes

13. Call to Renew Covenant

14. Command the Morning, Day and Night

15. Community Liberation and Solemn Assembly

16. Comprehensive Deliverance

17. Confront and Conquer Your Enemy

18. Contemporary Politicians' Prayers for Nation Building

19. Crossing the Hurdles

20. Dangerous Decrees to Destroy Your Destroyers (Series)

Free Book Gift

Just to say Thank You for getting my book: Christian Eschatology – Study 2, I'll like to give you these books for free:

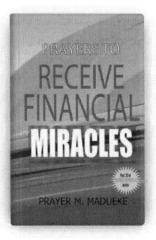

Click here to download these books now

If you're reading this from the paperback version, email me at prayermadu@yahoo.com.

Your testimonies will abound. Click here to see my other books. They have produced many testimonies and I want your testimony to be one too.

An Invitation to Become a Ministry Partner

In response to several calls from readers of my books on how to partner with this ministry, we are grateful to provide our ministry's bank details.

Be assured that our continued prayers for you will be answered according to God's word. And as you remain faithful by sowing seeds of faith, God will never forget your labors of love in Christ.

Send your Seed to:

<u>In Nigeria & Africa</u>

Bank Name: Access Bank

Account Name: Prayer Emancipation Missions

Account Number: 0692638220

<u>In the United States & the rest of the World</u>

Bank Name: Bank of America

Account Name: Roseline C Madueke

Account Number: 483079070578

Routing Number (RTN): 021000322

Visit the donation page on my website to donate online:
<u>www.madueke.com/donate</u>.